Sanctuary Map

CW00472024

A = Basilica of Our Lady (
B = House of Our Lady of Sorrows
C = House of Our Lady of Carmel
D = The Great Holm-oak. Under this same tree the
    children would await for Our Lady to appear.
E = The Capelinha – the Chapel of the Apparitions.
    The Position of the statue marks the spot where
    Our Lady actually appeared.
F = The Recinto
G = The Jubilee Wall
H = Pius XII Square

  1 = Basilica Sacristy
  2 = St Joseph's Chapel
  3 = Recinto Altar
  4 = Holy Family Chapel
  5 = Sanctuary Bookshop
  6 = Holy Angel's Chapel
  7 = Our Lady of Sorrows Chapel
  8 = Candle Pyre
  9 = The Sanctuary Information Centre
10 = Pius XII Monument
11 = Paul VI Monument
12 = Penitential Way
13 = High Cross
14 = First Bishop of Leria-Fatima Monument
15 = The Berlin Wall
16 = Sanctuary Administration Offices
17 = Nativity sculpture
18 = Chapel of reconciliation/Confessions
19 = The Sacred Heart Monument

Map of Sanctuary © José Manuel Braga

A PILGRIM'S HANDBOOK
TO FATIMA

Dedicated to

Mary Immaculate

The surest guide a pilgrim can have.

A PILGRIM'S HANDBOOK TO FATIMA

Leo Madigan

Gracewing.

First published in 2001

Gracewing
2 Southern Avenue, Leominster
Herefordshire HR6 0QF

ISBN 0 85244 532 6

Typeset by
Action Publishing Technology Ltd,
Gloucester, GL1 5SR

Printed in England by
MPG Books Ltd.,
Bodmin PL31 1EG

Contents

Front cover: The crown of Our Lady of Fatima (see pp. 43–44)
Back cover: The Golden Rose (see p. 24)

I wish to express thanks for assistance given in the preparation of this book to Teresa Marvão and Franco Cibabene who gave of their time and experience, and to Paul MacLeod of Geelong, Australia, who corrected my spelling with a persistence that bordered on martyrdom. Senhora Laura Pinheiro generously went over the original manuscript and made many valuable suggestions which I have implemented. Senhor José Manuel Braga of Lisbon gave unstintingly of his expertise in the preparation of the maps.

Mention is also due to SESDI for information and permission to use photographs from their archives.

The sections on the Sanctuary, and on the sites complementary to the Shrine, are greatly indebted to Chapter Two of the *Santuário de Fátima*'s official *Guia do Peregrino de Fátima*, (3rd edition, 1997).

Introduction

In the eighty plus years since Lucia dos Santos and Francisco and Jacinta Marto saw a beautiful lady in the Cova da Iria who told them that She came from heaven, years which have seen the Cova grow from a piece of rocky land with scant pasture to one of the major pilgrimage sites in the world, there hasn't been a comprehensive, factual guidebook to it in the English language – or indeed in any language, it seems, except the *Santuário*'s official *Guia do Peregrino de Fátima* in Portuguese. So, until the Baedeker of Fatima appears, I hope this offering will serve as a *vademecum*, not only to the bricks and mortar of the Sanctuary and the town, but to the message of Fatima, and to the spirit of Our Heavenly Mother who came here Herself to deliver it.

Compiling a guide to a religious shrine is not quite the same as getting one together for, say, the Palace of Westminster or downtown Manhattan. Curiosity is not a feature here. Fame, or splendour or value against the gold exchange are not criteria. This is not the same as saying that there is nothing curious about Fatima, that fame, or splendour or money have had no part in her development. It means that these material things, when they are met here, are secondary.

Fatima is the place that heaven chose to speak to

earth. It is the twentieth century's Sinai. It is the message that gives the place significance. For the individual pilgrim the only importance Fatima has is the message – that it is received, that it is understood, that it is taken to heart and acted upon.

One essential of the message is prayer. The form of prayer advocated by Our Lady, when She spoke at the Cova da Iria, is the Rosary.

The other essential of the message is penance. Penance should never be a negative thing. It isn't just a matter of not eating eclairs, but of willingly eating humiliation too – the lure is in discovering the inexplicable sweetness of aligning one's will with God's.

But the guide mustn't aspire to be the preacher. However, he must advise his party that Fatima is neither a museum nor a theatre. If the simple words of the message – prayer and penance – revolt you, or anger you, or are meaningless, it is better to go elsewhere until you feel more amicably disposed. The blind don't visit galleries nor the deaf concerts. It is true that on occasions miracles are worked here, but God won't work a miracle where no miracle is wanted. It is not the nature of Love to impose.

✝

Many facets of the Shrine are mentioned in this book several times in different sections. This crossing and recrossing of paths is inevitable in a handbook. We have tried to be as comprehensive as possible in the index so that no information sought by the pilgrim will be missed.

✝

A Brief History of the Shrine of Fatima

It is assumed that anyone coming in contact with this guide will already be familiar with the Fatima story, and perhaps already with the Cova da Iria. However, for the record, we briefly recount here the story of the Fatima apparitions followed by a list of principal dates in the development of the Shrine.

Fátima, village and sanctuary, Vila Nova de Ourém municipality, Santarém district, central Portugal pop. 10,000 (approx.); it is located on the tableland of Cova da Iria, 18 miles (29 km) south-east of Leiria and approximately 1000 ft (330 metres) above sea level. Named for a twelfth-century Moorish princess, Fátima has since 1917 been one of the greatest Marian shrines in the world, visited by millions of pilgrims annually.

THE ANGEL

In the spring, summer and autumn of 1916 three peasant children, Lucia dos Santos aged ten and her cousins Francisco (aged nine) and Jacinta Marto (aged seven), saw an Angel while tending the family flocks.

The first time was a on a rocky hillock called *Loca*

do Cabeço. Over the olive trees they saw approaching them a young man, about fourteen or fifteen years old, as white as snow, of great beauty and made as transparent as crystal by the sun. As he came close he said, **'Fear not, I am the Angel of peace. Pray with me.'** Kneeling on the ground till his forehead touched it, he told the children to repeat these words three times, **'My God I believe, I adore, I hope and I love You! I ask pardon of You for those who do not believe, do not adore, do not hope and do not love You.'** After rising the Angel said, **'Pray thus. The Hearts of Jesus and Mary are attentive to the voice of your supplications.'** Then he disappeared but the spiritual atmosphere which surrounded the children was so intense that for a long time they were not conscious of their own existence, remaining in the position the Angel had left them, constantly repeating the same prayer.

In the summer the children were playing near a well in the kitchen garden of Lucia's parents when the Angel appeared again and said, **'What are you doing? Pray! Pray very much! The Hearts of Jesus and Mary have designs of mercy on you. Offer prayers and sacrifices constantly to the Most High.'** Lucia asked how they could do that. **'Make of everything you can a sacrifice, and offer it to God as an act of reparation for the sins by which He is offended, and in supplication for the conversion of sinners. You will thus draw down peace upon your country. I am its Guardian Angel, the Angel of Portugal. Above** all, accept and bear with submission the suffering which the Lord will send you.' The Angel's words sank into their souls like a gleaming torch, showing them who God was, what His love for them was, how He wanted them to love Him in return; the value of sacrifice and how it pleases Him and how He receives it for the conversion of sinners.

In the autumn the Angel appeared again at Loca do Cabeço. The children immediately fell to their knees with their foreheads on the ground and repeated the *Believe, Adore, Hope and Love* prayer. After many repetitions they were aware of a strange light shining over them. Lifting their heads they saw the Angel holding a chalice in his left hand while over it, in the air, was a host. Drops of blood were falling from the host into the chalice. The Angel left the chalice and the host suspended in the air, knelt with the children and taught them to repeat three times, '**Most Holy Trinity, Father, Son and Holy Spirit, I adore You profoundly, and I offer You the most precious Body, Blood, Soul and Divinity of Jesus Christ, present in all the tabernacles of the world, in reparation for the outrages, sacrileges and indifference with which He Himself is offended. And, through the infinite merits of His most Sacred Heart, and the Immaculate Heart of Mary, I beg of You the conversion of poor sinners.**' The Angel rose, took the chalice and the Host in his hand, gave the Host to Lucia and the contents of the chalice to Jacinta and Francisco saying, '**Take and drink the Body and Blood of Jesus Christ horribly**

3

outraged by ungrateful men. Repair their crimes and console your God.' Bowing to the ground once more he repeated three times the *Most Holy Trinity* prayer and then disappeared. Overwhelmed by the supernatural atmosphere that surrounded them, the children continued to imitate the Angel in everything, kneeling prostrate as he had done and repeating the prayers he had taught them.

THE LADY

Sunday 13th May 1917.

On 13th of the following May the children were playing on the top of a slope (where the Basilica stands today) when they saw something like a flash of lightning. Thinking a storm was approaching they drove their sheep down the slope. Halfway down there was another flash and there stood a lady on top of a sapling oak tree, about a metre high. She was dressed in white, shining brighter than the sun, giving out rays of clear and intense light, like a crystal goblet full of pure water when the fiery sun passes through it.

They stood astounded in the light that radiated from her. She said, '**Do not be afraid. I will do you no harm.**'

Lucia asked, 'Where are you from?'

'**I am from heaven.**'

'What do you want of me?'

'**I have come to ask you to come here for six**

4

months in succession, on the 13th day, at this same hour. Later on, I will tell you who I am and what I want. Afterwards, I will return here yet a seventh time.'

'Shall I go to heaven too?'

'Yes, you will.'

'And Jacinta?'

'She will go also.'

'And Francisco?'

'He will go there too, but he must say many rosaries.'

'Is Maria das Neves, in heaven?'

'Yes, she is.'

'And Amelia?'

'She will be in purgatory until the end of the world. Are you willing to offer yourselves to God and bear all the sufferings He wills to send you, as an act of reparation for the sins by which He is offended, and of supplication for the conversion of sinners?'

'Yes, we are willing.'

'Then you are going to have much to suffer, but the grace of God will be your comfort.'

Then the Lady opened Her hands pouring a very intense light onto them, penetrating their hearts and the depths of their souls, showing them themselves in God. God Himself was the light, and they saw themselves much more clearly than in the finest mirror.

The lady said, **'Pray the Rosary every day, in order to obtain peace for the world, and the end of the war.'** Then She rose slowly into the east until

She disappeared into the immense distance. The light that encircled Her seemed to make a way among the stars which the children later described as the heavens opening.

Wednesday 13th June 1917.

The children were praying the Rosary as they waited. Again there was the light they called lightning and Our Lady was standing on the little oak tree.

Lucia said, 'What do you want of me?'

'I want you to come here on the 13th of next month, to pray the Rosary every day, and to learn to read. Later, I will tell you what I want.'

Lucia asked for the cure of a sick person.

'If he is converted he will be cured during the year.'

'I would like to ask you to take us to heaven.'

'Yes, I will take Jacinta and Francisco soon. But you are to stay here some time longer. Jesus wishes to make use of you to make me known and loved. He wants to establish in the world devotion to my Immaculate Heart. I promise salvation to those who embrace it, and those souls will be loved by God like flowers placed by me to adorn His throne.'

'Am I to stay here alone?'

'No, my daughter. Are you suffering a great deal? Don't lose heart. I will never forsake you. My Immaculate Heart will be your refuge and the way that will lead you to God.'

Once more She opened Her hands and communicated to the children the great light with which She was surrounded. In it they saw themselves as if submerged in God: Jacinta and Francisco seemed to be in that part which was rising to heaven and Lucia in that which was spreading over the earth. In front of the palm of Our Lady's right hand was a heart encircled with thorns which appeared to pierce it. They understood that it was the Immaculate Heart of Mary, calling for reparation for the outrages of humanity.

Friday 13th July 1917.

At the next apparition (by this time three or four thousand people had gathered around them) Lucia asked again, 'What do You want of me?'

'I want you to come here on the 13th of next month, to continue to pray the Rosary every day in honour of Our Lady of the Rosary, in order to obtain peace for the world and the end of the war, because only She can help you.'

'I would like to ask You to tell us who You are, and to work a miracle so that everybody will believe that You are appearing to us.'

'Continue to come here every month. In October, I will tell you who I am and what I want, and I will perform a miracle for all to see and believe.'

Lucia had been asked to intercede for some sick people. Our Lady replied gently that She would cure some but not others. Everyone must say the Rosary as a general condition for the reception of Grace. Of a sick man in Atouguia who asked to be taken soon to heaven She replied, '**Tell him not to be in a hurry. I know very well when I shall come to fetch him.**' Then She said, '**Sacrifice yourselves for sinners, and say many times, especially whenever you make some sacrifice:** *O Jesus, it is for love of You, for the conversion of sinners, and in reparation for the sins committed against the Immaculate Heart of Mary.*'

As in May and June Our Lady opened Her hands. The reflection they gave out seemed to penetrate the earth and they saw a sea of fire and plunged in this fire devils and souls like transparent embers, black or bronzed, in human form, which floated in the fire and were carried by the flames which they themselves gave forth, together with clouds of smoke, falling on all sides – as sparks fall in great fires – without weight or equilibrium, amidst cries of pain and despair which horrified the children and made them tremble with fear. The devils could be distinguished by their horrible and terrifying forms of strange, unknown animals, but transparent like burning coal.

Lucia gasped, went as pale as death, then cried out in terror to Our Lady, calling Her by name. She told them, kindly but sadly, '**You have seen hell where the souls of poor sinners go. To save them, God wishes to establish in the world devotion to my Immaculate Heart. If what I say to you is done, many souls will be saved and there will be peace. The war is going to end; but if people do not** cease offending God, a worse one will break out during the pontificate of Pius XI. When you see a night illumined by an unknown light, know that this is the great sign given to you by God that he is about to punish the world for its crimes, by means of war, famine, and persecutions of the Church and of the Holy Father.

'To prevent this, I shall come to ask for the consecration of Russia to my Immaculate Heart and the Communion of Reparation on the First Saturdays. If my requests are heeded, Russia will be converted, and there will be peace; if not, she will spread her errors throughout the world, causing wars and persecutions of the Church. The good will be martyred, the Holy Father will have much to suffer, various nations will be annihilated. In the end, My Immaculate Heart will triumph. The Holy Father will consecrate Russia to me, and she will be converted, and a period of peace will be granted to the world. In Portugal, the dogma of the Faith will always be preserved.'

[Here follows what was for long known as the third secret. In the words of Cardinal Sodano: It is a prohetic vision similar to those found in Sacred Scripture, which do not describe with photographic clarity the details of future events, but rather synthesise and condense against a unified background events spread out over time in a succession and duration which are not specified. The result must be interpreted in a symbolic key.

This is the official text of the letter written by
Lucia on 3rd January 1944 referring to the third part
of the 'secret' revealed to the seers on 13th July
1917.

I write in obedience to you, my God, who
commands me to do so through His excellency the
Bishop of Leiria and through your Most Holy
Mother and Mine.

After the two parts which I have already
explained, at the left of Our Lady and a little
above, we saw an angel with a flaming sword in his
left hand; flashing, it gave out flames that looked
as though they would set the world on fire; but
they died out in contact with the splendour that
Our Lady radiated towards him from her right
hand: pointing to the earth with his right hand, the
angel cried out in a loud voice: 'Penance, Penance,
Penance!'. And we saw in an immense light that is
God: 'something similar to how people appear in a
mirror when they pass in front of it' a Bishop
dressed in white 'we had the impression that it was
the Holy Father'. Other Bishops, Priests, men and
women Religious going up a steep mountain, at the
top of which there was a big Cross of rough-hewn
trunks as of a cork tree with the bark; before reach-
ing there the Holy Father passed through a big city
half in ruins and, half trembling with halting steps,
afflicted with pain and sorrow, he prayed for the
souls of the corpses he met on his way; having
reached the top of the mountain, on his knees at
the foot of the big Cross he was killed by a group
of soldiers who fired bullets and arrows at him,
and in the same way there died one after another

the other Bishops, Priests, men and women Religious, and various lay people of different ranks and positions. Beneath the two arms of the Cross there were two Angels each with a crystal aspersorium in his hand, in which they gathered up the blood of the Martyrs and with it sprinkled the souls that were making their way to God.

Cardinal Sodano said that the 'Bishop clothed in white who falls to the ground, apparently dead under a burst of gunfire is a prophecy of the attempt on the life of Pope John Paul II in Rome on 13th May 1981.' The Pope himself has spoken of 'a motherly hand which guided the bullet's path enabling him to halt at the threshold of death.' In reference to this prophecy Cardinal Ratzinger wrote, 'The future is not, in fact, unchangeably set, and the image which the children saw is in no way a film preview of a future in which nothing can be changed.'

'Do not tell this to anybody. Francisco, yes, you may tell him.' (Francisco was never able to hear what either the Angel or Our Lady said.)

When you pray the Rosary, say after each mystery: O my Jesus, forgive us, save us from the fire of hell. Lead all souls to heaven, especially those who are most in need.

After a silence a still terrified Lucia asked, 'Is there anything more that you want of me?'

'No, I do not want anything more of you today.'

As usual She rose towards the east and disappeared into the firmament.

11

Sunday 19th August 1917. Valinhos.

No apparition took place at Cova da Iria on 13th
August because the Administrator of the Municipality, Artur de Oliveira Santos, had arrested the
children and taken them to Vila Nova de Ourém with
the idea of forcing them to reveal the secret. He
imprisoned them in his own home and in the munici-
pal jail. They were offered all manner of attractive
presents if they would reveal the secret. The children
refused, saying that they would prefer death. He made
them believe that a vat of olive oil was being heated to
boil them alive if they did not obey him. They were
adamant in their refusal until finally, on the morning
of 15th August he returned them to the Fatima pres-
bytery.

On 19th, around 4 o'clock in the afternoon, Our
Lady appeared to the shepherds at Valinhos between
Aljustrel and Loca de Cabeço. Lucia, as usual, asked
what it was that Our Lady wanted.

'I want you to continue going to the Cova da
Iria on the 13th, and to continue praying the
Rosary every day. In the last month, I will
perform a miracle so that all may believe. If
they had not taken you to the town the miracle
would have been greater.'

'What do you want done with the money people
leave in the Cova da Iria?'

'Have two litters made. One is to be carried by
you and Jacinta and two other girls dressed in
white; The other is to be carried by Francisco

12

and three other boys. The money from the litters is for the *festa* of Our Lady of the Rosary, and what is left over will help towards the construction of a chapel that is to be built here.'

Lucia asked for the cure of several invalids.

'Yes, I will cure some of them during the year. Pray, pray very much, and make sacrifices for sinners; for many souls go to hell, because there are none to sacrifice themselves and to pray for them.'

Our Lady then arose and ascended towards the east.

Thursday 13th September 1917.

In September, twenty-five to thirty thousand people had assembled at the Cova da Iria. When Our Lady appeared she repeated her request for them to say the Rosary and again foretold the October apparitions. She added, 'Our Lord will come, as well as Our Lady of Dolours and Our Lady of Carmel. St Joseph will appear with the Child Jesus to bless the world. God is pleased with your sacrifices. He does not want you to sleep with the rope on, but only to wear it during the daytime.'

Lucia said, 'I was told to ask you many things, the cure of some sick people, of a deaf mute ...'

Yes, I will cure some, but not others. In October I will perform a miracle so that all may believe.

Our Lady rose towards the east. Many of the people saw a luminous sphere rising in that direction.

Saturday 13th October 1917.

An immense crowd, estimated at over seventy thousand, were in the Cova da Iria when the children arrived. It was said that when Our Lady appeared at midday a misty cloud like incense enveloped the group as Lucia asked the customary, 'What do you want of me?'

'I want to tell you that a chapel is to be built here in my honour. I am the Lady of the Rosary. Continue always to pray the Rosary every day. The war is going to end, and the soldiers will soon return to their homes.'

'I have many things to ask you: the cure of some sick persons, the conversion of sinners, and other things ...'

'Some yes, but not others. They must amend their lives and ask forgiveness for their sins. Do not offend Our Lord any more, for he is already so much offended.'

Having said this She rose and, opening Her hands as she had in May, June and July, threw beams of light towards the sun. The crowd saw the black clouds draw apart like a torn curtain to reveal the sun as a luminous disc, in colour like the blade of a knife, not dazzling the eye. According to the father of Francisco and Jacinta the sun seemed to flicker on and off, first one way, then another. It shot rays in different directions and painted everything in different colours, the trees, the people, the air and the ground. Then the sun seemed to stop and then begin to move and to dance until it seemed that it was being detached from the sky and falling on the people.

Maria Carreira, a local lady from Moita who looked after the site, said that the sun turned everything different colours, yellow, blue, white, and it shook and trembled. It seemed like a wheel of fire which was going to fall on the people. They cried out, 'We shall all be killed! We shall all be killed!' Others called to Our Lady to save them and recited acts of contrition. One woman began to confess her sins aloud. At last the sun stopped moving and everybody breathed a sigh of relief. They were still alive and the miracle which the children had foretold had taken place.

It seems that different people saw different things, though the activity of the sun was a central experience. Many saw rose petals falling, as had also been reported in September, and others were enveloped in the brilliance of the changing colours. Mabel Norton, a non-Catholic Englishwoman in service in Portugal who was present 'saw the sun describe a swift circle, pause, describe another, pause again and describe a third. Then the clouds began to sweep over it again. Someone pulled my sleeve. It was an ancient crone, her face alight. "Do you see the roses falling?" she asked. She saw them, but for me, there in the mud, there were no roses, only a sense of disappointment. I had hoped for, half expected, a vision, compelling, all-powerful, such as St Paul saw on the road to Damascus; something that would change one's life completely. Perhaps this was presumption, perhaps just ignorance. What it was makes no difference, neither does what I felt or thought. Our Lady knew Her people.'

The children also saw something quite different, a series of tremendous visions, tableaux which seemed to represent the Joyful, Sorrowful and Glorious Mysteries of the Rosary. Lucia said: 'After Our Lady had disappeared in the immense distance of the firmament, we beheld St Joseph with the Child Jesus and Our Lady robed in white with a blue mantle, beside the sun. St Joseph and the Child Jesus appeared to bless the world, for they traced the Sign of the Cross with their hands. When, a little later, this apparition disappeared, I saw Our Lord and Our Lady; it seemed to me that it was Our Lady of Dolours. Our Lord appeared to bless the world in the same manner as St Joseph had done. This apparition also vanished, and I saw Our Lady once more, this time resembling Our Lady of Carmel.'

Wednesday 16th June 1921.

At two o'clock in the morning as she was departing in secret for the Dorothea Sisters' convent boarding school at Asilo de Vilar near Porto, the fourteen-year-old Lucia stopped to say the Rosary at the chapel which had been built at Cova da Iria. Here, it is said, Our Lady appeared to her for the seventh time, as she had originally promised.

Thursday 10th December 1925. Pontevedra, Spain.

On 10th December 1925 when Lucia was in her room

on the second storey of the Dorothean convent in Pontevedra, Spain, the Most Holy Virgin appeared to her and, by her side, elevated on a luminous cloud, was a Child. The Most Holy Virgin rested Her hand on Lucia's shoulder and as She did so She showed her a heart encircled by thorns which She was holding in Her other hand. At the same time the Child said, **'Have compassion on the Heart of your Most Holy Mother, covered with thorns, with which ungrateful men pierce it at every moment, and there is no one to make an act of reparation to remove them.'**

Then the Most Holy Virgin said, **'Look, my daughter, at My Heart, surrounded with thorns with which ungrateful men pierce me at every moment by their blasphemies and ingratitude. You could console Me by making it known that all those who, for five (consecutive) months, go to confession, receive Holy Communion, say the Rosary and keep Me company meditating for fifteen minutes on the fifteen mysteries of the Rosary with the intention of consoling Me. I promise to help them at the hour of their death with all the graces necessary for salvation.'**

Thursday 13th June 1929. Tui (Tuy) Spain.

For an account of this apparition see *The Consecration of Russia to the Immaculate Heart of Mary* in the section 'FATIMA DEVOTIONS', p. 139.

FRANCISCO

In December 1918 Francisco fell ill with the Spanish influenza which was ravaging Europe and is said to have caused the death of more people than the First World War. He was confined to bed in his family home in Aljustrel where he offered his sufferings to console Our Lord.

On 3rd April 1919 he made his first Confession and Holy Communion. At 10 a.m. the following day he silently passed away. His mother said, 'His face lit up in a smile as he drew his last breath.' His father said simply, 'He died smiling.' He was buried in the Fatima cemetery. On 12th September 1935 Jacinta's body was brought from a private tomb in Ourém so that the two would be interred together in the Fatima cemetery in a specially prepared tomb. On 13th March 1952 his mortal remains were transferred to a tomb in the southern transept of the Basilica.

He was beatified along with his sister on 13th May 2000. His feast day is celebrated along with Jacinta's, on 20th February, because the day of his death which would normally be his feast day would often occur in Easter week and therefore would rarely be celebrated.

JACINTA

Jacinta came down with the Spanish influenza a month or so before Francisco in October 1918. The course of her illness was erratic and she was sometimes able to get up. She would spend those days sitting with Francisco. On one occasion she sent for Lucia and told her, 'Our Lady came to see us. She told us She would come to take Francisco to heaven very soon, and She asked me if I still wanted to convert more sinners. I said I did. She told me I would be going to a hospital where I would suffer a great deal; and that I am to suffer for the conversion of sinners, in reparation for sins committed against the Immaculate Heart of Mary, and for love of Jesus. I asked if you would go with me. She said you wouldn't, and that is what I find hardest. She said my mother would take me, and then I would have to stay there all alone!'

And that is what happened. On 31st October 1919 she was taken to Ourém Hospital and later, on 21st January 1920, to Lisbon where she was admitted to Mother Godinho's Orphanage in Estrela. On 2nd February she was taken to Dona Estefânia Hospital where she died on 20th February 1920, at 10.30 p.m. Her body was taken back to Ourém by train and buried in the family vault of Baron Alvaiázere. On 12th September 1935 when it was transferred to the tomb built for her and Francisco in the Fatima cemetery, the body was found to be perfectly incorrupt. On 1st May 1951 it was transferred to a grave in the nothern transept of what was then the new Basilica in Cova da Iria. A grave to accommodate Lucia's body after her death has been prepared beside it.

Along with Francisco she was beatified on 13th May

2000 and, as has been said, her feast day is celebrated on the day of her death, 20th February.

LUCIA

After several years as a boarder in the school of the Dorothean Sisters in Vilar, near Oporto, Lucia joined the Dorothean congregation and, on 25th October 1925, was sent as a postulant to their convent in Pontevedra in Spanish Galicia, north of the Portuguese border. Her name with the Dorotheans was Sister Dores (Sorrows). Later she was moved to the Sisters' convent in Tuy, a border town on the Spanish side of the Minho river. She made her first profession here on 3rd October 1928. Many years later, on 27th May 1946, she was posted to the College of the Sacred Heart of Jesus of Sardão in Vila Nova de Gaia across the river from Oporto.

Having obtained permission from Pius XII to take up the contemplative life she entered the Carmelite Convent in Coimbra on 25th March 1948 with the name Sister Mary of the Immaculate Heart. On 23rd March 2001 she will be ninety-four years old.

Principal Dates
28.4.1918?: The building of the Capelinha das Aparições in the Cova da Iria is started by the local people, neither encouraged nor discouraged by the Church authorities.

13.5.20: Gilberto Fernandes dos Santos, from Torres Novas, orders a statue of Our Lady of Fatima which is made by José Thedim and delivered to Fatima. On 13.6.20 it is placed in the Capelinha.

13.10.21: Mass is permitted for the first time in the Capelinha das Aparições.

5–6.3.22: The chapel is dynamited, apparently with the connivance of the authorities. Maria Carreira had taken the statue to her home the previous evening to protect it from the damp. A parochial procession of reparation in which 10,000 people take part is followed on 13.2.22, by a National Pilgrimage of Reparation attracting 60,000 people from all over Portugal. The capelinha is restored between 13.12.22 and 13.1.23. The open-sided covering was added on 13.10.24.

3.5.22: The Bishop of Leiria orders an investigation into the events at Cova da Iria.

13.10.22: The first number of the *Voz de Fátima*, the official paper of the Cova da Iria, is issued.

13.6.22: The first Blessing of the Sick takes place.

10.5.23: The Civil Governor of Santarem prohibits all pilgrimages on 13th. He sends the Republican Guards to implement his orders. They are not carried out. Many of the Guards join in the Rosary.

13.1.24: The first Mass is celebrated in the Capelinha.

13.10.24: The foundation stone for the Hostel for the Sick is laid.

1.11.26: Mons. Nicoltra, the Apostolic Nuncio, is invited for the installation of the first Bishop of Leiria.

26.6.27: The Bishop of Leiria, at an official ceremony at the Cova da Iria, blesses the Stations of the Cross which are placed at intervals on the 12 kilometre road up the mountain from Reguengo do Fetal.

13.7.27: A first rector of the Sanctuary is appointed.

13.5.28: The foundation stone for the Basilica, a block of white marble, is laid by the Bishop of Evora. Work on the Basilica is begun.

12.5.29: Salazar and other members of the government visit the shrine. In Rome, on 6.12.29 Pius XI blesses the statue of Our Lady of Fatima offered by the sculptor, José Thedim, to the Portuguese College there.

1.10.30: Papal indulgences granted to the faithful making pilgrimages to Fatima.

13.10.30: *By the Provision of Divine Providence* the Bishop of Leiria declares the apparitions *worthy of belief* and officially authorises the cult of Our Lady of Fatima.

13.5.31: The first consecration of Portugal to the Immaculate Heart of Mary by the Portuguese Episcopate.

12.9.35: Jacinta's coffin is brought from Ourém for reburial with Francisco in a specially prepared tomb in the Fatima cemetery. Both bodies are present in the Chapel of Confessions (since demolished) where Mass is celebrated by the Archbishop of Evora.

13.9.39: The Bishop of Leiria makes public Our Lady's request to Lucia concerning the Five First Saturdays.

7-13.4.42: Silver Jubilee year of the Apparitions. Triumphal departure of the Statue to preside at Catholic Youth Congress in Lisbon. The women of Portugal promise Our Lady a Crown of Jewels to thank Her for keeping Portugal out of the war.

31.10.42: Pius XII, speaking in Portuguese on the radio, consecrates the world to the Immaculate Heart of Mary.

13.5.46: The coronation of the statue of Our Lady of Fatima in the Capelinha das Aparições by Cardinal Masella, the Papal Legate. Representing the President of Portugal, the Minister for the Interior hands the crown to the Cardinal on behalf of the women of Portugal. Such a vast crowd is present that the gates of the Sanctuary have to be shut to prevent further ingress. A medal is struck to commemorate this great occasion.

July 1946: British Catholics in Portugal offer a beautiful gold chalice to Our Lady of Fatima in thanks and remembrance, for when the bombing of London was at its height, the Mothers of Portugal journeyed to Fatima to pray for the Mothers of Britain. Our Lady heard their prayer and the bombing died away.

22.11.46–24.12.46: The statue is taken to Lisbon in solemn procession for the feast of the Immaculate Conception. (See 'Doves of Bombarral' p. 174.)

7.10.49: The Irish Monstrance is presented to the Shrine by Finbar Ryan OP, Bishop of Port of Spain in Trinidad. A group of four hundred and fifty Irish pilgrims travel overland to attend the event. (See 'Irish Monstrance' p. 168.)

13.10.51: The official closing of the Holy Year, in Fatima, by Cardinal Tedeschini, the Papal Legate.

7.10.53: The Basilica is consecrated.

13.5.56: Cardinal Roncalli, Patriarch of Venice and future Pope John XXIII, presides at the ceremonies for the anniversary pilgrimage.

21.11.64: Pope Paul VI announces the granting of the Golden Rose to the Sanctuary. It is delivered the following May by the Papal Legate, Cardinal Cento.

13.5.67: Pope Paul VI comes to Fatima on the fiftieth anniversary of the first apparition of Our Lady. A crowd estimated at one million gathers to attend the Papal Mass and to pray for peace.

10.7.77: Pilgrimage to Fatima of Cardinal Luciani, the future Pope John Paul I.

13.5.82: The Holy Father, John Paul II, comes in pilgrimage to Fatima in gratitude to Our Lady for having saved his life during the assassination attempt on this day the year before. He consecrates all Men and Nations to the Immaculate Heart of Mary.

25.3.84: The Holy Father John Paul II renews the Consecration of the World to the Immaculate Heart of Mary in St Peter's Square in the Vatican before the statue of Our Lady of Fatima from the Capelinha das Aparições. Sister Lucia confirms that this dedication meets Our Lady's request.

13.5.91: Pope John Paul II again visits Fatima on the tenth anniversary of the attempt on his life in St Peter's Square by gunman Ali Agci.

13.5.2000: Francisco and Jacinta Marto are beatified in Fatima during the third visit of Pope John Paul II to the Shrine. At the end of the Mass Cardinal Sodano, on behalf of the Holy Father and in the presence of Sr.

Lucia and up to a million pilgrims, reveals the essence of the third part of the 'secret' which Our Lady had revealed in July 1917. The full text of the 'secret' was published by the Vatican on 26.6.2000. (See p. 10)

A Pictorial History of Fatima

1917. Local Council map of the Cova da Iria before the Apparitions. Most plots are called Cova of something, or simply marked by the name of the owner. The individual plots were delineated by low stone walls.

The 70,000 gather before midday in the rain in the Cova da Iria on 13th October 1917, the day of the miracle of the sun.

A closer view of the crowd still waiting in the rain on 13th October 1917.

13th October 1917. Lucia had told the crowd to shut their umbrellas and say the Rosary.

13th October 1917. Lucia, under the guidance of an interior impulse, had cried out to the people to look at the sun. Note that the moustached man half-seen standing at the far right of the picture is the same man who is towards the left of picture no. 4, kneeling next to the young man with the staff who is looking at the camera.

The 13th May pilgrimage in 1922. The partial destruction of the roof and walls of the Capelinha was a result of the dynamiting during the night of 6th March 1922 by enemies of the faith.

1931. Entrance portico and columns which at that time limited the area of the Sanctuary. They stand approximately where the wall was built for the AD 2000 Jubilee.

1931. Inside the Capelinha. Note the votive offerings beneath the roof, left in gratitude for requests granted. The José Thedim statue is still in its niche above the altar.

Olympia and Ti Marto, the parents of Francisco and Jacinta, receive a blessing in their doorway. The priest on the left is possibly Dr Ludwig Fischer (see p. 215).

1932. On 13th May 1932 the statue of the Sacred Heart of Jesus on its plinth above the fountain was inaugurated. The building behind the monument is the original Chapel of Confessions.

1937. The Capelinha with its *alprende* (constructed awning), and the fountain.

1937. The Recincto with the Central Avenue, as it was called, the fountain with the Sacred Heart monument, the Capelinha, the Chapel of Confessions, and the Basilica under construction.

1938. The first phase of the construction of the modern Cova da Iria.

Aerial view in 1938, taken from the roof of the Basilica which was still without its bell tower.

Another aerial view of the Sanctuary on 13th October 1951. This was also the official closing of the extended 1950 Holy Year – a ceremony which officially took place in Fatima. The High Cross, just visible in the centre foreground, is the monument erected to mark the event.

13th May 1953. Note that the four large statues of Portuguese saints are in place above the colonnades, but not the thirteen smaller statues.

Picture taken on 13th May 1957.

An Explanation of Some Portuguese Nouns

A number of nouns are used in their Portuguese form throughout this handbook. These nouns, and their English equivalents, are explained here.

Aljustrel
Is the name of the village where the *dos Santos* and *Marto* families lived. It is about two kilometres to the south of the *Santuário*. Apart from most of the village houses now being used to cater for visitors (and life for the villages would probably be intolerable if they weren't) *Aljustrel* can't be much different from what it was at the time of the apparitions. There are very few modern buildings in evidence and the council hasn't streamlined the roads. It is relatively easy to drive into from the Minde Road, the EN360, but a bit of a maze to drive out of, given the necessary one-way system. The best way to approach it is on foot from the Southern Roundabout, the *Rotunda Santa Teresa de Ourém*, up the *Via Sacra*.

Capela
Capela is easily recognised as the word for 'chapel'. Its etymology is interesting. When St Martin of Tours divided his military cloak – *cappa* in Latin – in the

fourth century and gave half to the beggar at the gate of Amiens, he wrapped the other half around his shoulders thus making a cape – *capella*. This cape, or its representation, afterwards accompanied the Frankish kings in their wars and the tent which sheltered it also became known as the *capella*. In this tent Mass was celebrated by the military chaplains – *capellani*. Subsequently any oratory where Mass was celebrated was called *capella* or, in French, *chapelle*.

Capela da Reconciliação
The Chapel of Reconciliation. A collection of oratories and confessionals beneath the South Colonnade.

Capelinha
Little chapel. In Fatima *Capelinha* almost always refers to the *Capelinha das Aparições*, the Chapel of the Apparitions, the open chapel, on the north side of the vast concourse, which houses the tiny original chapel and the statue of Our Lady of Fatima.

    inha or *inho*, *zinha* or *zinho* added to a word in Portuguese creates a diminutive. Thus *irmã*, sister, becomes *irmãzinha* as in *As Irmãzinhas de Jesus*, The Little Sisters of Jesus. Similarly *obrigado*, thank you, can become *obrigadinho*, thanks.

Cova da Iria
This might be translated as the Dip or Hollow of Peace. *Cova* is a bit slight to be a cave (*gruta*). It is sometimes rendered as hole, or pit or even coffin. The local *Camara* (Council) map of the area for 1917 shows

many sections called *Cova* – *Cova do Cebolo* (onion-seed), *Cova da Machado* (axe) *Cova das Tormentas* (of the torments).

Iria, although it could mean 'it makes irridescent' probably comes from the Greek meaning 'peace' from where we get the English word 'irenic' – promoting peace. The Greek goddess Irene was the goddess of peace (the Romans called her Pax) which passed into the girl's name Irene. There were several Saint Irenes, one being a Portuguese nun who died around AD 635. Her name is immortalised in Portugal in the city Santarem. (Say Saint Irene – pronounce it to rhyme with 'keen' – ten times quickly and you are saying Santarem as a Portuguese might say it.)

Cruz Alta

The High Cross. The cross at the western end of the *Recinto*. It was erected to mark the closing of the Holy Year 1951. (1950 was actually the Holy Year but it was extended into 1951.)

Fátima

Although the whole area is known in Portugal and world wide as Fatima, the *Santuário* and the town that has grown up around it is, properly speaking, the *Cova da Iria*. *Fátima* itself is about two kilometres away on the EN365, the *Vila Nova de Ourém* road leading off the *Rotunda Santa Teresa de Ourém*. The original parish church is its centre. Two pre-apparition villages, *Moita Redonda* (circular copse) and *Lomba d'Égua* (mare's plateau) to the north and east

30

of Cova da Iria are virtually incorporated into the main township. However, they both have their own chapels – *Moita* has *Stª Luzia* and *Lomba d'Égua*, *S. João*.

Fátima Parish Church is still the parish church for the whole area, which is why all the other churches (apart from the Basilica) are called chapels. (Chapels of Ease, is the traditional English language expression, the idea being to 'ease' the strain on an overburdened church.)

For the purposes of clarity this guide will use the Portuguese *Fátima* (acute over the first 'a') for the original village of *Fátima* and the International Fatima (without acute) for the entire shrine and surrounding area.

The origin of the word Fátima as a Portuguese village is interesting. It is well known as the name of the Islamic prophet Muhammad's daughter. The story goes that in 1158 (In England, Henry II was on the throne and Thomas á Becket, later Saint, was his Chancellor) a high ranking party of the Moorish occupiers were ambushed while they picnicked on the banks of the river Sado, south of the Tagus. The captives were taken to the Portuguese king, Alphonso Henriques, in Santarem. During the journey the leader of the Christian knights, Gonçalo Hermingues, became enamoured of one of the young women of the party whose name was Fatima. He asked the king if he could take her as his wife. The king agreed providing Fatima herself consented, and that she became a Christian. Apparently Fatima returned Gonçalo's affection for she agreed on both counts and was given the name *Oureana* – the Golden One. The king's wedding gift was a village named *Abdegas* which took the name of its new mistress and which time has whittled down to *Ourém*. Oureana died young. The grieving Gonçalo joined the Cistercian monastery of *Alcobaça* and after some time the abbot had Oureana's body transferred to a grave in monastic lands not far from the couple's village and built a small commemorative chapel there which, probably because her Christian name was already in use, became known by her former, Muslim name, Fatima.

Some see a Muslim name being used as the name of one of the great shrines of Christendom as ironic. 'What could be more pleasing in these troubled times,' runs a well known comment, 'than to see Catholics praying to a Jewish mother in a place named after Muhammad's eldest daughter.' Indeed, when Iranian Television broadcast a film of pilgrims walking the Penitential Way on their knees, the commentary told its viewers that the pilgrims were Catholics paying homage to Islam.

Others see it as underlining the universality of the Blessed Virgin's message. Prayer, penance, eschatalogical truths are hardly the preserve of Catholics alone. It would seem presumptuous to hold that Our Blessed Mother's appearance in Fatima, rather than any one of a dozen more Christian sounding places within a few kilometres, was an oversight.

Fonte or Fontenário

This refers to the area in the centre of the esplanade, hedged and fenced in iron, where the statue to the Sacred Heart stands on a plinth.

The whole of the area of the Fatima parish was notorious for its lack of artesian water. Even when diviners' rods shook and wells were dug little more than a trickle would result, and not even the trickles were regular. There appears to have been a body of water called the Carreira Pond for the livestock. (This pond lay opposite the first station of the Via Sacra near the South Roundabout, the Rotunda de Stª Teresa de Ourém. On 5th April 1999, a marble plaque was set on the site to commemorate it.) There was little else in the way of water, however, apart from the unreliable domestic wells.

As pilgrims flocked to the site of the apparitions the Bishop, while making no statement on their credibility or otherwise, first permitted Mass to be celebrated in the Cova and then bought the land so that it would not be profaned. As the number of pilgrims increased the lack of water became an urgent problem and the Bishop commissioned a cistern to be built so that water could be brought in and stored in it. On 9th November 1921 workmen arrived with picks and shovels to dig a hole in the dry, rocky earth to accommodate the cistern and no sooner had they struck it than water sprang up.

The water was channelled into a circular, arched fountain house with fifteen outlets but this was covered over when the Recinto was levelled in 1950.

(A second spring had emerged in 1927, five yards away from the first.) There are now four outlets for the water around the circular hedge which encloses the Sacred Heart statue and many others among the surrounding parks.

Lausperene
Perpetual praise. This refers to the chapel of Perpetual Adoration of the Blessed Sacrament at the end of the east colonnade.

Loca do Cabeço or Loca do Anjo
Loca do Cabeço (the top of the hill) is the name given to a cave on a rocky knoll; the knoll itself is known as *Cabeço*. *Cabeço* and its cave are a little north of Aljustrel. A corner of it, which Lucia in her memoirs calls *Chousa Velha* (old 'small inheritance'), a favourite gazing spot for the little shepherds, was the site of the first and third apparition of the angel in the spring and the autumn of 1916. For this reason *Chousa Velha* is now called *Loca do Anjo* (Place of the Angel). A group of marble statues stands among the rocks, the three children kneeling in front of the angel.

Procissão de Velas
The candlelit procession which is held in the Sanctuary every night at 21.30 hrs during the summer months. Possibly the most enduring memory of the Shrine for pilgrims when they have returned to their homes is the Rosary and procession of worshippers, each holding a lighted candle and following the

flower-bedecked statue as it is carried around the precinct. (On Thursdays it is the Blessed Sacrament which is carried in procession.) At the beginning of the Rosary the candles are blessed by the presiding cleric.

On the Capelinha schedule which is displayed on the notice boards each day this devotion is abbreviated to 'tv'. This doesn't mean that the Rosary and procession is televised; tv here stands for *terço* (q.v.) *com velas*.

During the winter months the Rosary is recited in the Capelinha at 21.00hrs. If enough of the faithful are present a candlelit procession will also be held.

Procissão do Adeus

The Farewell Procession. One of the most moving sights in Fatima must be when the statue of the Virgin, which has been taken to the Recinto Altar for Mass, is being borne back to the Capelinha. It is then that the entire assembly bursts into a display of affection and waves white handkerchiefs as the statue is carried down the steps and along the middle of the esplanade. (Take two handkerchiefs, veteran pilgrims advise – one to wave and one to dab your tears.) What many foreign pilgrims can't understand is why handkerchiefs are waved at the statue after some Masses and not after others.

The answer to the puzzle is that the Portuguese pilgrims are not waving because the statue is going away, it is because they themselves are. It is part of the way of life for Portuguese families to come to Fatima by car, by coach, by foot or whatever on Friday or Saturday and to stay over until the Sunday, then head back for home after the midday Mass. Hence the wave to the statue representing Our Lady. This farewell is also reflected in the words of the hymns sung during the Procissão do Adeus – the *Senhora Nós Vos Louvamos* ('Hossana, Hossana, Queen of Portugal') and the *Ó Virgen do Rosário*, ('O Fatima, goodbye; Virgin Mother, goodbye').

Recinto
Precinct, esplanade. This word refers in general to the vast concourse between the Basilica and the *Cruz Alta*. When a Mass or a liturgical function is announced as being held in the Recinto it means the *Altar of the Recinto* which is the glassed-in chancel on the steps in front of the Basilica.

Although it has been likened to a military parade ground and an airport runway, the area, which is twice the size of the *piazza* in front of St Peter's in Rome, is packed to capacity on the days and nights of the May and October pilgrimages. Few sights can be as inspiring as the sight of the *Recinto* during a vigil Mass, when hundreds of thousands of people, all holding lighted candles, are assembled there in prayerful silence.

Santuário
Sanctuary. The area from the Basilica to the Paul VI Centre including *Nossa Senhora do Carmo* and *Nossa Senhora das Dores*. It is also sometimes used to cover

the *Reitoria* in general, the management of the shrine. If someone is said to be staying in the *Santuário* they will be staying in the Casa Nossa Senhora do Carmo building.

Terço
Is five decades of the Rosary i.e. a third. The full fifteen decades is called a *Rosário*.

Pista dos Penitentes
The Penitential Way. The marble path leading from the Pilgrim Statue of Paul VI near the Cruz Alta down to, and encircling, the *Capelinha das Aparições*. Pilgrims show their conformance with the wishes of Our Lady for penance by negotiating this path on their knees. When there is no Mass or public devotion being held in the Capelinha many pilgrims cover the last part of the penitential walk inside the low walls of the Capelinha sanctuary.

The genesis of this practice is told in Lucia's memoirs. The time is shortly after the Cova da Iria apparitions:

'My mother fell so seriously ill that, at one stage, we thought she was dying. All her children gathered round her bed to receive her last blessing, and to kiss the hand of their dying mother. As I was the youngest, my turn came last. When my poor mother saw me, she brightened a little, flung her arms around my neck and, with a deep sigh, exclaimed, "My poor daughter, what will become of you without your mother! I am dying with my heart pierced through because of you."

37

Then, bursting into tears and sobbing bitterly, she clasped me more and more tightly in her arms.

'My eldest sister forcibly pulled me away from my mother, took me to the kitchen and forebade me to go back to the sick room, saying, "Mother is going to die of grief because of all the trouble you've given her!" I knelt down, put my head on a bench, and in a distress more bitter than any I had ever known before, I made the offering of my sacrifice to our dear Lord. A few minutes later, my two sisters, thinking the case was hopeless, came to me and said, "Lucia! If it is true that you saw Our Lady, go right now to the Cova da Iria, and ask her to cure our mother. Promise her whatever you wish and we'll do it; and then we'll believe."

'Without losing a moment, I set out. So as not to be seen, I made my way across the fields along some bypaths, reciting the Rosary all the way. Once there, I placed my request before Our Lady and unburdened myself of all my sorrow, shedding copious tears. I then went home, comforted by the hope that my beloved Mother in heaven would hear my prayer and restore health to my mother on earth. When I reached home my mother was already feeling somewhat better. Three days later, she was able to resume her work around the house.

'I had promised the most Blessed Virgin that, if she granted me what I asked, I would go there for nine days in succession, together with my sisters, pray the Rosary, and go on our knees from the roadway to the holm oak tree; and on the ninth day we would take nine poor children with us, and afterwards give them

38

a meal. We went, then, to fulfil my promise, and my mother came with us.'

Those making the penitential way are strongly advised to wear knee pads, which may be bought from shops near the sanctuary – ask for *joelheira*, they cost around 550 escudos – and to remember to carry their beads to pray the Rosary while negotiating the marble path from the Pope Paul VI statue, through the Jubilee Wall down the incline of the Sanctuary Precinct and around the Capelinha.

Via Sacra

The Stations of the Cross. There are three outdoor public Stations of the Cross in the Fatima area. One is on the walls of the colonnade on either side of the Basilica. This is usually referred to as *Via-sacra, na colunata*. The second is the *Via Sacra e Calvário* which winds up through the olive groves from the South Rotunda, by-passes Aljustrel and finishes at the chapel of St Stephen (*Capela de Santo Estêvão*) with the three crosses and four figures of Calvary above it and known as the Hungarian Calvary (*Calvário Húngaro*).

The third *Via Sacra* starts at Reguengo do Fetal and finishes in the Praça St José at the main open northern entrance to the Sanctuary. This Via Sacra consists of fourteen large stone crosses which were erected and inaugurated by Bishop José de Silva on 26th June 1927. (Another branch of this *Via Sacra* starts at Torre, just north of Reguengo do Fetal, traverses the hills there, turns south at Pedrulheira, Lucia's mother's village, and joins the main Fetal Stations at

Vale de Ourém for the Eight Station where they continue as one.) The crosses were the gift of the surrounding parishes.

The Sanctuary

When Our Lady appeared in 1917, the Cova da Iria was a rural property owned by Lucia's parents and which they eventually gave to the Sanctuary. The nearest villages, Moita Redonda and Lomba d'Égua, lay about a kilometre away, as the crow flies. The entire Sanctuary grew up from the tiny Chapel of the Apparitions, built by the people, without any participation whatsoever from the ecclesiastical authorities.

In the desire to help the pilgrim spend time fruitfully in Fatima here are some notes which may be useful. But please! Don't inconvenience anyone during your visit, and especially those who are at prayer.

The Sanctuary of the Cova da Iria

Built gradually following the apparitions of Our Lady, the Sanctuary is situated in the area of the township of Fatima, but the actual place itself is called Cova da Iria. Cova da Iria was the name of that area of the countryside in which the apparitions of Our Lady took place and which was owned by the parents of Lucia. Iria means *peace*, which points to the nature of the message, indeed seems to be a sign from a divine source, showing the basic purpose of the Sanctuary.

The original level of the Cova da Iria was deeper than at present. It was five metres below the actual pavement where the statue of the Sacred Heart of Jesus stands, and 340 metres above sea level.

The Sanctuary is composed of the Chapel of the Apparitions, the Precinct of Prayer, the Basilica and columns, the Retreat houses of Our Lady of Carmel (with the Rectory area) and Our Lady of Sorrows (with an area for the sick), Pius XII Square and the Paul VI Pastoral Centre.

The Chapel of the Apparitions

A chapel was built in the place of the Apparitions in 1919; it was begun on 28th April and completed on 15th June. The building of the chapel was in response to the request of Our Lady, 'I want you to build a chapel here in honour of Our Lady of the Rosary.'

The first Mass was celebrated here on 13th October 1921. It was partly dynamited on the night of 5–6th March 1922 and was restored between 13th December 1922 and 13th January 1923.

In 1982 a large three-walled area was built. It was inaugurated during the visit of Pope John Paul II on 12th May that year. In 1988, the Marian year, its ceiling was lined with Russian pinewood brought from the north of Siberia. This wood was chosen for its durability and lightness. The original chapel, which has been decorated to remove the signs of wear over the years, still keeps the characteristics of a popular shrine.

The pedestal, on which can be seen the image of

Our Lady, marks the exact spot where the little holm oak grew (it disappeared owing to the devotion of the first pilgrims who took it away branch by branch), a metre or so in height, on which Our Lady appeared to the shepherds on 13th May, June, July, September and October 1917.

The Statue
The statue of Our Lady which is venerated in the chapel was donated, in 1920, by Gilberto Fernandes dos Santos, of Torres Novas. It was blessed in the Fatima Parish Church on 13th May 1920 by the parish priest, Father Manuel Bento Moreira, and set up in the chapel on 13th June in the same year. It is the work of a devout sculptor José Ferreira Thedim. It is made of wood, Brazilian cedar, and measures 1.10 metres. It was restored by the sculptor in 1951 and has been refurbished at various times since. On 13th May 1946 it was solemnly crowned by the Papal Legate, Cardinal Masella.

When the Blessed Virgin appeared to the children She was not wearing a crown but the people have always crowned Her statues in Her honour. The precious crown, which the statue only wears on the days of major pilgrimage, was given by the women of Portugal on 13th October 1942. It is gold, weighs 1.2 kilos and is encrusted with 313 pearls and 2,679 precious stones. It is a unique example of the high artistic value of the jeweller's craft.

The statue has left the Sanctuary eight times. The first was in 1942 when it was taken to the church of

Our Lady of Fatima in Lisbon, and the seventh was on 25th March 1984, when it went to Rome where Pope John Paul II solemnly consecrated the world to the Immaculate Heart of Mary in St Peter's Square. On the same day the Pope offered to the Sanctuary the bullet which was used in the attempt on his life on 13th May 1981 and which was incorporated into the crown on 26th April 1989. The eighth time was for the weekend of 8th October 2000 when it was again taken to Rome where the Holy Father, John Paul II, consecrated the Millennium to the Immaculate Heart of Mary.

Other Statues of Our Lady of Fatima
The Pilgrim Virgin
In addition to the statue of Our Lady of Fatima in the Chapel of the Apparitions there appeared, in the 40s, another by the same sculptor which, as it was made under suggestions from Sister Lucia, is considered more in accord with the apparitions of 1917. Beginning from the moment it started out on its world travels on 13th May 1947 this statue came to be known as the *Pilgrim Virgin*. In September 1947 it was in the Dutch city of Maastricht after which it passed through Spain, France, Belgium, and Luxembourg. To date it has travelled through almost all the world including the countries of Eastern Europe, and notably Russia. From the beginning of the journeys the statue was copied and enthroned in thousands of churches the world over.

The Statue of the Immaculate Heart of Mary

Supported by new revelations of Sister Lucia, about the apparition of 13th July 1917 in which Our Lady showed her Immaculate Heart, new statues were carved under this title, the first of which, by the same sculptor, José Thedim, can be found in the Carmel of Coimbra.

On 13th May 1958 the inauguration took place of a great statue of the Immaculate Heart of Mary. It was made by Father Thomas McGlynn, OP, under the direction of Sister Lucia and placed in a niche in the façade of the Basilica on 3rd June 1959. It is 4.70 metres high and weighs 14 tons. The Rosary in Our Lord's right hand is the work of Dominican nuns in the United States and is made of ivory.

This image, a gift of the Catholics of America, evokes the substance of the message referring to the devotion to the Immaculate Heart of Mary, which Our Lady gave in the first three apparitions at the Cova da Iria and in the apparitions of Pontevedra: the devotion to the five first Saturdays, the Consecration of Russia, and the triumph of her Immaculate Heart.

Images of the Fatima Immaculate Heart of Mary are also spread throughout the whole world.

The Great Holm-Oak Tree

This holm-oak was already a mature tree in the Cova da Iria in 1917. Because of its function in the life of the seers it has its part in the history of the apparitions. Lucia speaks of it when describing the first apparition on 13th May 1917. In the following months it was under the shadow of this oak that the three shepherds prayed the Rosary with the people who accompanied them, while awaiting the appointed time of the apparitions. The plaque against the wall surrounding the tree reads:

THE GREAT HOLM-OAK

UNDER THIS TREE THE YOUNG SHEPHERDS
PRAYED WHILE THEY WAITED FOR OUR LADY.
THE OAK OF THE APPARITIONS WAS SITUATED
IN THE PLACE WHERE TODAY THE
SMALL COLUMN (AND STATUE)
IS FOUND BENEATH THE GREAT WOOD AND GLASS
AWNING   ·
COVERING THE CAPELINHA.

The Colonnade and the Way of the Cross
This is the mirror architecture which joins the Basilica to the buildings on either side of the precinct. It is the work of the architect António Lino and comprises two hundred columns and fourteen altars.

The mosaics in the alcoves behind the altars are the fourteen Stations of the Cross, in polychrome ceramics, designed by Lino António, (this is not a printer's error; the name of the artist mirrors the name of the architect) and made by the *Viúva Lamego* factory in Lisbon. In June 1955 the rough sketches, pictures, and two of the panels were put on public exhibition. A Leira journal later commented: *In the panel of the burial of Jesus, the intimate drama which the figure of*

Our Lord, and the suffering of the Holy Women communicates, would move the hardest heart to compassion. And what can be said of the aching tenderness of Joseph of Arimathea for the Lord? In the crucifixion panel the movement of the soul which the painter makes the agents of the tragedy assume is noteworthy – and look at the hammers and nails! Only a 'painter familiar with the mysteries of religion' (as Diogo de Macedo, an art authority called Lino António) is able to interpret the intimate drama of each figure.

The Statues of the Saints

Above the colonnade are to be found seventeen marble statues representing Portuguese saints, saints who founded religious congregations represented in Fatima, and other apostles of devotion to Mary. (For biographies of these saints see p. 217)

The four major statues, measuring 3.20 metres, and representing Portuguese saints are:

1. Saint John of God, founder of the Order of the Hospitalers of St John of God and patron of hospitals, nurses and the sick. The sculptor was Alvaro Brée.
2. Saint John de Brito, a Great Apostle of Mary in the seventeenth century, sculpted by António Duarte.
3. Saint Anthony of Lisbon (*aka* Saint Anthony of Padua), Doctor of the Church, canonised one year after his death in 1231. The sculptor was Leopoldo de Almeida.

4. Blessed Nuno of Saint Mary (Nuno Álvares Pereira). He was beatified in 1918. The sculptor was Barata Feio.

The smaller statues measure 2.30 metres and can be found spreading out in a semi-circle from the Basilica. From left to right, facing the Basilica, they are:

1. Saint Teresa of Ávila.
2. Saint Francis de Sales.
3. Saint Marcellin de Champagnat.
4. Saint John Baptist de La Salle with pupil.
5. Saint Alphonsus Maria de Ligouri.
6. Saint John Bosco with Saint Dominic Savio.
7. Saint Louis Maria Grignion de Montfort.
8. Saint Vincent de Paul.
9. Saint Simon Stock.
10. Saint Ignatius Loyola.
11. Saint Paul of the Cross.
12. Saint John of the Cross.
13. Saint Beatrice da Silva.

The Basilica

Exterior
The Basilica arose in the place where, on 13th May 1917, the three little shepherds were playing a game of 'making a wall'. Suddenly there was a flash which they thought was lightning, and they began to herd their flock together to return to their homes.

The project was conceived by the Dutch architect Gerard van Kriechen and continued by the architect João Antunes. On 13th May 1928 the first stone was blessed by the Bishop of Évora, D. Manuel da Conceição Santos. The consecration was on 7th October 1953. The title of *Basilica* was granted by Pius XII in the brief *Luce Superna* on 12th November 1954.

The building, which measures 70.5 metres long and 37 metres wide, was built totally with local stone from Moimento, and the altars are made of marble from Estremoz, Pero Pinheiro and from Fatima.

The bell tower rises in the centre of this assembly of buildings. It stands 65 metres high and is completed by a bronze crown weighing 7,000 kilos. This crown was cast in the foundry of Bolhão, Porto. In 1999 it was restored and completely covered in gold. On the very top is an illuminated cross which, at night, can be seen from a long way off. This, too, was renewed in 1999.

The carillon is composed of 62 bells, cast in Fatima by José Conçalves Coutinho of Braga. The main bell weights 3,000 kilos and its clapper 90. The clock is the work of Bento Rodrigues of Braga.

The angels of the facade are of marble and are the work of Albano França.

The statue of the Immaculate Heart of Mary in the niche of the tower is, as has already been noted, 4.70 metres high and weighs 14 tons. It was sculpted by Fr. Thomas McGlynn, OP.

At the entrance to the Basilica, above the main door,

can be found a mosaic which represents the Most Holy Trinity crowning Our Lady. It was made in the Vatican and was blessed there by the then Secretary of State, Cardinal Eugénio Pacelli, the future Pope Pius XII, the 'Pope of Fatima'.

The Nave

Not stylish, but elegant in the simplicity of its lines, the temple consists of a great nave, a transept and two sacristies, one of which was converted into a place of worship and called the Chapel of Saint Joseph.

The Basilica has fourteen side altars, each of which represents a mystery of the Rosary in bronze bas-relief, the work of Martinho de Brito, and later gilded by Alberto Barbosa. The fifteenth mystery is represented in stone in the vault of the Main Church, showing the Most Holy Trinity crowning the Most Holy Virgin. It is in high-relief and is the work of the sculptor, Maximiano Alves.

The stained-glass of the side altars, which represent some of the invocations of the Litany of Our Lady, and those in the rest of the galleries, the part above the nave and the transept, and likewise all the paintings of the interior, are the work of João de Sousa Araújo. They show scenes referring to the life of Our Lady, to the Apparitions and to the message of Fatima. They date from 1967.

The cross arch, made in the Vatican, shows a mosaic over its full span spelling out the words *Regina Sacratissimi Rosarii Fatimae ora pro nobis.* (Queen of the Most Holy Rosary, pray for us.) It was a gift of the

Catholics of Singapore, and it records, too, the dedication of the Basilica of Our Lady of the Rosary, the
name by which the Lady called herself on 13th
October 1917.

The Chancel

Behind the balustrade an image of Our Lady of Fatima
is exposed for the veneration of pilgrims.

In 1995 this building was renovated as a chancel by
the architect Erich Corsepius. In the centre is a great
stone altar which takes the place of the original altar.
Its front is silver and is considered a work of art. It was
made by Jewellery Alliance of Porto, and represents
the Last Supper of Christ.

The pulpit, the new pedestal for Our Lady and the
celebrant's throne are made of the same stone as the
altar.

In the wall on the left side can be found a bronze
medal with the effigy of D. José Alves Correia da
Silva, first Bishop of the restored diocese of Leiria
(1920–1957) whose mortal remains lie here.

The picture behind the altar is the work of the
painter João de Sousa Araújo and represents the
message of Our Lady coming in the form of light and
of peace, to meet with the seers, prepared by the Angel
and after their encounter with Christ in the Eucharist.

The Church is present at this meeting in the person
of the Bishop of the diocese who is kneeling on the
left.

In the upper right hand corner the Popes who
received and took part in the message are represented:

Pius XII who sent his legate, Cardinal Masella, to crown Our Lady of Fatima and consecrate the world to the Immaculate Heart of Mary:

John XXIII who visited the Sanctuary before he became Pope:

Paul VI who came to Fatima in 1967 and who proclaimed Our Lady Mother of the Church, sealing this decision with a gift of a Golden Rose for the Sanctuary.

On the opposite side, three angels contemplate this message of the Mother of God to men, a Message of prayer, of penitence, of reparation and of hope.

The stained glass windows in the Main Church represent: the four evangelists; the apparition of the angel; a scene from the life of the shepherds; and aspects of the Cova da Iria on pilgrimage days. They are the work of the society *Maumejean y Hijos* of Madrid.

On the side pillars of the Main Church there are two stones with inscriptions celebrating the coronation of Our Lady of Fatima on 13th May 1946, and of the Closing of the Holy Year on 13th October 1951.

The Tombs of the Seers

On the extreme right of the transept is the tomb of the seer Blessed Francisco Marto, who died on 4th April 1919. On the wall behind the tomb is an image of the seer seated in a tree with a lamb on his lap. The birds in the representation remind us that Lucia in the *Memoirs* tells that he was very fond of birds and always kept part of the bread he had for his lunch, breaking it into crumbs and spreading them out on the top of the rocks. 'And they,' she writes, 'keen-eyed as they are, did not wait for the invitation, but came flocking around him. It was his delight to see them flying back to the tree tops with their little craws full, singing and chirping in a deafening chorus, in which Francisco joined with rare skill.' This wall sculpture was commissioned for the beatification of Francisco on 13th May 2000.

The painted panels represent the Bishop of Leiria-Fatima and the three seers, encircled by the cord which they used as an instrument of sacrifice for the conversion of sinners and about which Our Lady told them: **'God is pleased with your sacrifices, but He doesn't want you to sleep with the cord.'**

On the opposite side is the tomb of the seer, Blessed Jacinta Marto, who died on 20th February 1920. In February 1995 another tomb was opened next to it to hold Sister Lucia, following an agreement between the Carmel of Coimbra and the Sanctuary of Fatima.

The wall sculpture behind Blessed Jacinta's tomb, also commissioned for the 13th May 2000 beatification, shows Jacinta standing among hills holding a sheep in her arms. This also is taken from Lucia's Memoirs.

'Jacinta, what are you doing there,' I asked her, 'in the middle of the sheep?'

'I want to do the same as Our Lord in that holy picture they gave me. He's just like this, right in the middle of them all, and he's holding one of them in his arms.'

The two panels which are placed under the altars relate to the life of Jacinta, and to the Church.

On 13th May 1989 the Holy Father signed a decree proclaiming the heroic virtue of the two servants of God, Francisco and Jacinta. Following an attested miracle, involving the medically unexplainable cure of a Leiria woman, Maria Emília dos Santos, Francisco and Jacinta were beatified by Pope John Paul II in Fatima on 13th May in the Jubilee year 2000. Their joint feast day is 20th February.

Statues

On the right side of the nave there is a statue of St Domingos de Gusmão, or, in English, St Dominic, the founder of the Dominican order of Friars Preachers and a great apostle of the Rosary in the twelfth century. The sculptor was Maria Amélia Carvalheira da Silva.

On the left side is St Anthony Maria Claret, founder of the Congregation of the Missionary Sons of the Immaculate Heart of Mary. The statue is the work of Martinho de Brito.

At the end of the Basilica, on the right-hand side as one enters, is a statue of St John Eudes, a holy Frenchman of the seventeenth century, a great preacher, founder of the Congregation of Jesus and Mary, and of the Congregation of Our Lady of Charity of the Refuge. It is also the work of Martinho de Brito.

On the left side is St Stephen, first King of Hungary who, in the year 1000, consecrated his nation to Our Lady. This image was the gift of Hungarian Catholics and commemorates the suffering of the Hungarian people for their faith when their country was invaded by Russia. It is the work of António do Amarel de Paiva.

The Organ

The organ was built and assembled by the firm Fratelli Rufatti of Padua in 1952. The five parts of the instrument were originally located independently, but they were reunited in 1962 in the choir loft. These five parts, the Grand Organ, the Positive, the Recitative, the Solo and the Echo are individual functions of one console which has five keyboards and pedals. It has 152 registers and approximately 12,000 pipes which are made of lead, tin and wood. The largest of these are 11 metres, the smallest 9 millimetres.

The Chapel of St Joseph

This is entered through the sacristy or by an external door on the left side of the Basilica. The five stained glass windows of this chapel are the work of Eduardo Nery. They rise in a harmony of colours and geometric figures and symbolise the five first numbers 1, 2, 3, 4 and 5.

The Chapel of Perpetual Adoration

Situated at the base of the colonnade, on the left side as one comes out of the Basilica, the present chapel of the Holy Perpetual Adoration (*Lausperene*) was inaugurated on 1st January 1987. It was built as a gift from the Austrian Association *Crusade of Reparation by*

Means of the Rosary for the Peace of the World and the first stone was blessed by Pope John Paul II on 13th May 1982.

The architect was J. Carlos Laureiro. The two stained glass windows at the entrance represent the manna in the desert and the Last Supper. They are the work of the artist Orlanda Sá Nogueira. The silver monstrance is the work of the sculptor Zulmiro de Carvalho.

From 1st January 1960 the Most Blessed Sacrament has been exposed and adored, day and night, in the Sanctuary of Fatima, this being the third Chapel of Perpetual Adoration. The perpetual vigil of Adoration is undertaken by the Reparation Sisters of Our Lady of Sorrows of Fatima. The Chapel is open to the public from 7 a.m. till 11 p.m.

The Administration Offices and the Retreat House of Our Lady of Carmel

Alongside the Chapel of Perpetual Adoration, on the southern side of the precinct, we find the Rectory and administration offices of the Sanctuary occupying the ground floor and two basements of the Nossa Senhora do Carmo building. This structure was rebuilt and remodelled from 1982 under the architect J. Carlos Loureiro and inaugurated by the Cardinal Patriarch of Lisbon, D. António Ribeiro on 13th May 1986.

In the entrance hall of the Rectory stands a statue of Our Lady sculpted by Teixeira Lopes in 1931.

Above and behind the Rectory is the Retreat House of Our Lady of Carmel, with 210 beds, a refectory, two chapels (Our Lady of Carmel with 130 seats and Holy Spirit with 70 seats) and assembly rooms (Our Lady of Carmel – 210 seats, Anjo de Portugal – 90 seats, Holy Spirit – 60 seats, Salon 44–30 seats and six more salons for ten and fifteen people.)

The Popes stay here when visiting the shrine; Paul VI for 13th May 1967 and John Paul II on 12th–13th May 1982, 1991 and 2000. It is in this house, or sometimes in Our Lady of Sorrows, that the Portuguese Bishops' Conference meets several times during the year.

The Berlin Wall

In a south side-entrance to the Sanctuary a monument consisting of a concrete block from the Berlin Wall may be found. The construction of the Wall, decreed by the East German Volkskammer (People's Chamber) to isolate West Berlin as an island in the Eastern Communist State was started on the night of 12th–13th August 1961. Demolition started on 9th November 1989, a dramatic indication of the collapse of Communist rule promised by Our Lady as a result of the collegiate episcopal consecration to the Immaculate Heart which was made in Rome, 25th March 1984.

This block was given by a representative of Portuguese emigrants in Germany, Virgilio Casimiro Ferreira, and was established here in grateful recognition of the intervention of God, promised at Fatima, in the halt of communism. The block weighs 2,600 kilos, is 3.6 metres high and 1.20 metres wide. The setting of the monument is by the architect J. Carlos Loureiro. It was inaugurated on 13th August 1994.

Pius XII Square and the High Cross

Situated above the precinct, the area was given this name in homage to the Pope who, having been consecrated Bishop on 13th May 1917, gave testament at various times to his love of Fatima. The statue of Pius XII, by Domingos Soares Branco, was erected in 1961, with offerings from German Catholics.

In the centre-left of the square, facing the Basilica, is a monument to Paul VI in an attitude of prayer, the work of Joaquim Correia, in homage to the first Pope to visit Fatima – on 13th May 1967, the 50th anniversary of the first apparition of Our Lady.

In the centre-right is the High Cross, which is 27 metres tall and was designed by the architect Carlos Freire, to mark the closing, in Fatima, of the 1950 Holy Year. This took place on 13th October 1951 as the Holy Year was extended. During the ceremony the Papal legate, Cardinal Tedeschini revealed that the Holy Father, Pius XII, had himself been granted the sight of the Miracle of the Sun in the Vatican gardens the previous November, on the eve of the proclamation of the dogma of the bodily Assumption of the Blessed Virgin into Heaven.

On the right side, opposite the statue of Pius XII, is a statue of D. José Alves Correia da Silva, the Bishop of Leiria to whom it fell to declare that 'the visions of the children in the Cova da Iria are worthy of belief' (13th October 1930) and who officially allowed the cult of Our Lady of Fatima. The sculptor is Joaquim Correia.

The Penitential Way
or The Pilgrimage of the Knees

The board here reads:

Prayer Before Making the Pilgrimage of the Knees

Most Holy Trinity
Father, Son and Holy Spirit,
I adore you profoundly.
My heart rejoices in all
the benefits you have given me.
Help me to make reparation
For the evil of my sins.
Accept this pilgrimage of the knees
To the blessed place where Mary
Told us of the certainty of your love.

For this sacrifice
(And I hope to fulfil my promise to make it)
I implore the blessing of pardon
On poor sinners.
Finally may all people
Be open to the message of the gospel,
May we enjoy peace in the present,
And arrive one day at eternal joys
Through Christ Our Lord. Amen.

The Pavilion of Saint Anthony

This prefabricated structure was erected in 1992. It serves for the reunion of various groups from the Sanctuary and other institutions, namely the Music School, the House of Youth (the responsibility of the Message of Fatima Movement), the Anonymous Families Movement, Alcoholics Anonymous, and the National Secretariat of Clergy, Seminaries and Vocations. It has an exhibition hall.

The Precinct of Prayer

Moving in the direction of the Basilica we find the vast precinct, or *recinto*, of prayer, which we can think of as a great open-air church. It measures, together with Pius XII Square, 540 metres long and 160 metres wide. It has a surface of 86.400 m² and can hold more than half a million pilgrims. It is usually packed in May and August, uniting at those times one of the most fervent assemblies of the spiritual life in the world.

The Hostel and Retreat House of Our Lady of Sorrows

At the foot of the precinct we find low buildings behind the Capelinha, in which are included the Secretariat of the Message of Fatima Movement, the Information Office, the candle stalls and the pyre where the candles are burned.

Behind these buildings, and much higher than them is the hostel for the sick and invalids who come to Fatima on pilgrimage or retreat. Initiated in 1926 and later remodelled it received great improvements in its internal installations between 1992 and 1995 under the project of the architect J. Carlos Loureiro. It has 135 beds and a First Aid post with various consulting rooms and a small surgery.

In the central body of the building is the Chapel of Our Lady of Sorrows, with its great picture which symbolises the triumph of the Immaculate Heart of Mary, and a stained glass which represents the Miracle of the Sun. These two works are by the Italian artist P. G. Lerario of the Friars Conventuals. Popularly this space is known as the Chapel of the Sun. Before the present Lausperene, or Chapel of Perpetual Adoration, the Blessed Sacrament was exposed here for the adoration of the faithful.

Behind this area reserved for the sick is an even vaster space, the Retreat House, with 154 beds, refectories, two chapels (Immaculate Heart of Mary – 90 seats, and Holy Angels – 250 seats) and assembly rooms (Our Lady of Sorrows – 200 seats, John XXIII – 130 seats, Immaculate Heart of Mary – 45 seats, The Jacinta Room – 30 seats, and the Pius XII Room – 20 seats) and also the offices and assembly rooms of the Association of the Servants of Fatima. It serves to welcome sick and invalided and other people for retreats and spiritual activities.

Monument to the Sacred Heart of Jesus

This monument is found in the place where, on 9th November 1921, water appeared after some initial boring. The original fountain house with its fifteen basic spouts was demolished because of the levelling of the precinct, leaving only the upper part visible, and the column which supports the statue of the Sacred Heart of Jesus. Now there are four taps there accessing the spring.

This statue is of gilded bronze and the sculptor is unknown. It was the gift of a pilgrim and was blessed by Mons. Beda Cardinale, Apostolic Nuncio on 13th May 1932. Its location in the centre of the precinct marks the centrality of the person of Jesus in the message of Fatima, which was already clear during the apparitions of the Angel.

Jubilee 2000 Wall

To mark the 2000 Jubilee year the Sanctuary of Fatima, in its capacity of a Jubilee Sanctuary, constructed a wall at the main entrance to the Recinto.

The wall is an expression of the Evangelist's words, 'I am the door; by me if any man enter in, he shall be saved,' (John 10:9 King James and Douay versions) a text which is inscribed in fourteen languages on the side facing the Avenue and the Paul VI Centre. Also on this side are shallow pools with underwater lights which symbolise purification. On the two end surfaces of the walls facing each other across the opening the legend *Jubilæum 2000* appears vertically.

Inspired by this sentence of St John, the work is actually composed of two cement walls, symmetrical in relation to the Recinto but separated from each other. This space between them is the 'door'. This 'door' is open to the Santuario as a place of purification, yet it also symbolises Christ's warning that 'the gate is narrow and the way is hard that leads to life' (Matt. 7:13.). At the same time 'all things work together for good for those who love God.' (Romans 8:28.) For this reason the side of the wall facing the Basilica bears the words 'God is Love' in the various languages.

In the area of the 'door' a pavement of granite cobblestones has been laid creating a floor which is distinct from the surface of the rest of the Recinto. This represents a 'passageway' which affords the pilgrim a new and thought-provoking entrance to the Santuario of Fatima, providing a moment to pause and to help focus attention on the true meaning of the Fatima message.

The decision to make the Basilica of the Santuario of Fatima a Jubilee Church was taken by the Bishop of Leiria-Fatima, Dom Serafim Ferreira e Silva, in a pastoral letter on 13th July 1999, following the Papal Bull *Incarnationis Mysterium*, issued on the first Sunday of Advent 1998. According to this Pontifical document a plenary indulgence could be gained by visiting the Basilica during the Jubilee year with the usual conditions of sacramental confession, communion and prayer.

The Jubilee Wall was officially opened on 25th December 1999.

The Information Centre
There are now two information outlets provided by the Sanctuary. The established one is to the west of

the *Capelinha*, behind the candle pyre. The newer one is on the same side of the Sanctuary, at the top of the steps leading to the *Praça São José*. These are easily recognised by the signs *Acolhimentos* and *Informações*.

It is a pity that there is no word or phrase in English that translates *Acolhimento*. 'Information desk' is too abrupt, 'meeting place' is too clumsy, 'reception centre' is too impersonal. *Acolhimento* is a combination of all three, but with a fire in the corner, warm and welcoming. The 'Come you blessed of my Father ...' verses in the Gospel (Matt. 5. 34–35) where Christ announces what will be said to those for whom the gates of heaven are open tells, '... because I was hungry and you gave me food, I was thirsty and you gave me drink, I was a stranger and you took me in.' In Portuguese this last clause reads, '... *era Peregrino e me acolheste*,' which illustrates the flavour of the word *acolhimento* nicely.

The Sanctuary Information site was officially established on 1st August 1973, but the spirit of the centre existed long before that in the person of Mother Luisa Andaluz, the foundress of Fatima's own congregation of women Religious – the Servants of Our Lady of Fatima. Mother Luisa had always considered the welcoming of pilgrims and the answering of their questions to be an important part of her mission.

She sowed the seed and the seed grew to be the highly organised and expertly staffed arm of the Sanctuary that today greets the innumerable pilgrims who enter its doors each year. Most of the staff and volunteers speak English and take a genuine delight in answering questions, directing the enquirer in the right direction.

Mention must be made, too, of the eight page folding brochure on the Shrine that the Centre distributes, a superb summary of all the facilities of the Sanctuary – the essential foundation on which this *Fatima Handbook* is built. It would be difficult to name an international attraction anywhere, religious or secular, that provides such a well-produced and informative leaflet in a variety of languages, and provides it gratis.

Don't be shy about approaching the *Acolhimento e Informações*; it exists for you.

The Blessing of Vehicles

Drivers will benefit from the grace of having their vehicles blessed at the official Blessing of Vehicles which takes place twice each Sunday, at 12.45 and again at 16.30 throughout the summer months.

The area set aside for this short ceremony is the park behind the Sanctuary bookstore on the north side of the Sanctuary area. The entrance is on the right as one drives down from the Praça São José and has several signs at the entrance, one of which reads:

**Benção de Veiculos
neste espaço []
Domingos 12H 45
e
16H 30**

65

The Paul VI Pastoral Centre

Situated on the far side of the Avenue D. José Alves Correia da Silva is the Paul VI Pastoral Centre, named in memory of the Pope who, with his pilgrimage on 13th May 1967, honoured Fatima during the time of the Second Vatican Council.

It was built in response to the real pastoral needs of the Church and serves to house meetings, congresses, reunions etc. of a religious, cultural or scientific character. The inaugural stone was blessed on 13th May 1979 by Cardinal Franjo Seper, then Prefect of the Sacred Congregation of the Doctrine of Faith, and the Centre itself was inaugurated by Pope John Paul II on 13th May 1982. It is on four levels with an area of 14,000 square metres and is the project of the architect J. Carlos Loureiro, of Porto.

It has a grand amphitheatre with the capacity for 2,124 people seated, a dividable room which can hold around 800 people, three rooms for 80 people, five for 40 and an office. All the rooms are equipped with an internal video system and for the projection of 16 and 35 mm films. Also, on the basement and sub-basement levels, dormitories with 388 beds are available along with a self-service restaurant, all at modest prices for pilgrims, retreatants, lecture groups, but above all for young people.

In one of the corners of the entrance hall is a 'Little Shepherd' in bronze. It is the work of sculptor José Rodrigues. In the amphitheatre there is a 'Risen Christ' in bronze by Professor Lagoa Henriques. It is 3.40 metres high.

In the corridor leading to the Minor Salon a statue to Our Lady, Mother of the Good Shepherd, has been put up. It is made of Estremoz marble and is the work of the sculptor Graça Costa Cabral. The sculptor Maria Irene Vilar carved the wooden 'Christ Crucified' which is to be found in the Minor Salon.

The painter Julio Resende painted a stained glass in the chapel representing the Good Shepherd.

On the lawn in the front of the building is a statue of Our Lady by Domingos Soares Branco. For some years previously this statue was in front of the main entrance to the Sanctuary.

Sites Complementary to the Sanctuary

We call complementary those places and sites in the vicinity of the road taken by the seers when they went from Aljustrel to the Cova da Iria. These places are complementary in the sense that they are recognised as completing a visit to the Sanctuary proper, which is situated in the Cova da Iria. In fact, apart from being the natural habitat of the little shepherds, these places were sanctified by the three apparitions of the Angel of Peace and the fourth apparition of Our Lady.

The Way of the Cross and Calvary

This begins at the Roundabout of St Teresa of Ourém (Rotunda Sul) where in 1917 there was a pond (Lagoa da Carreira) from which the livestock drank. A plaque to this effect was erected here in 1999. Following the road trodden by the seers, the Way of the Cross finishes at the Chapel of St Stephen (The Hungarian Calvary). The fourteen Stations and the chapel, the gift of Hungarian refugees in the West, are the work of the Hungarian engineer Ladislau Marec and were inaugurated respectively on 11th August 1962 and 12th May 1964.

The panels of the Stations in bas-relief and the statue of Our Lady, Patroness of Hungary, are the work of the Portuguese sculptor Maria Amélia Carvalheira da Silva.

The eleven stained glass windows of the chapel, work of the Hungarian artist Pedro Prokop, represent the saints and the *beati* of Hungary. By the same artist are the two great mosaics of the ceiling (1994) which represent, respectively, the apparition of Our Lady surrounded by the seven sorrows and the surrender of the crown of Hungary by the king, St Stephen, to Our Lady who is surrounded by the seven joys. None of the stones in these mosaics is artifically coloured.

The Fifteenth Station, dedicated to the resurrection of Jesus was inaugurated on 13th October 1992, the twenty-fifth anniversary of the erection of the Way of the Cross properly so called. This Fifteenth Station was offered by the Hungarian parish of Lajosmizse, which was represented at the inauguration by the parish priest and a group of parishioners. Also present were two Hungarian bishops and the Hungarian Ambassador to Portugal. This offer was made as a sign of gratitude for the resurrection of Hungary following the end of the Cold War.

Cabeço

According to the recollections of Sister Lucia it was here that the second and third apparitions of the Angel to the little shepherds occurred. It was in this place that the angel taught them the prayer *Most Holy Trinity, Father, Son and Holy Spirit etc.* and gave them communion, inviting them to make reparation and offer consolation to the offended God.

The statues of the Angel and the three shepherds are the work of Maria Amélia Carvalheira da Silva. They were inaugurated in 1958. The rails, forged in iron, are the work of Soares Branco. Note how each frame forms a scene of the Fatima drama – the Miracle of the Sun, the Chalice and Host etc.

Valinhos

Between the Eighth and Ninth Stations of the Way of the Cross is the place of the Apparition of Our Lady around 4 p.m. on 19th August 1917. It was here that she made the appeal, carved on marble on the side of the path in front of the statue, '*Pray, pray very much, and make sacrifices for sinners, for many souls go to hell because there are none to pray and to sacrifice themselves for them.*'

The monument itself was built from offerings from Hungarian Catholics and inaugurated on 12th August 1956. The statue is the work of Maria Amélia Carvalheira da Silva and the niche of the architect António Lino.

The House-Museum of Aljustrel

Some hundreds of metres from Valinhos, next to the house of the birth of the seer *Lúcia de Jesus*, is the house-museum of Aljustrel which belonged to Maria Rosa, Godmother of Lucia. It was a centre for regional ethnography from 1969. Acquired by the Sanctuary of Fatima, it was reappointed and inaugurated on 19th August 1992.

Its intention is to show what village life was like at

the time of the apparitions. Various forms of employ-
ment are represented, shoemaking, dressmaking,
carpentering, weaving. In the yard is the bread oven,
the threshing floor, the mill storage. There is a black-
smith's shop with forge and anvil for horse-shoeing, a
stone-cutter and mason's workplace, stables, kitchen
and examples of typical bedrooms and reception
rooms.

This view of an almost lost way of life should be of
great interest to new generations. The entrance fee is
minimal and children are admitted free.

Lucia's House

It was here that *Lúcia de Jesus* came into the world, the
last of six children, on 22nd March 1907 and it was
here that the first 'historic' questioning of the seers
was made. Lucia lived here until she was fourteen at
which time she left for the Asilo (Shelter) de Vilar in
Porto – on 17th June 1921.

In the grounds are the fig trees under the shadows
of which the three cousins played, and where they hid
when they were being sought out by the curiosity of
strangers and pilgrims.

On 13th August 1994 an information post was inaugurated in the same grounds. Sister Lucia gave the
house to the Sanctuary on 17th November 1981.

The Well of Arneiro

The well of Arneiro (*Arneiro* means barren or sandy
land) is at the bottom of the kitchen garden behind

71

Lucia's house. It is notable because it is the site of the second apparition of the Angel of Portugal who told them that they should, *'Offer prayers and sacrifices to the Most High ... (making) of everything you can a sacrifice.'*

Also it was in this place that Jacinta, so devoted to the Vicar of Christ, had a vision of the Holy Father who was crying and praying in a great house, on his knees and with his face in his hands.

The House of Francisco and Jacinta
In the bedroom in front of the entrance door the brother and sister were born, Francisco on 11th June 1908 and Jacinta on 11th March 1910. In the bedroom to the left of the entrance, Francisco suffered his painful illness for over three months and it was here that he died, on 4th April 1919. Both were visited here by Our Lady. The house was acquired for the Sanctuary on 9th November 1996. It was restored, and officially reopened in time for the children's beatification.

The Parish Church and Cemetery
These are situated a kilometre to the east of Aljustrel and two kilometres from the Sanctuary. The church was renovated in 2000 and Sister Lucia visited this and other sites familiar to her childhood on 16th May 2000 before she returned to the Carmel of Coimbra after attending the beatification of her cousins.

At the entrance to the church, on the left side of the main entrance, is the baptismal font where the three shepherds were baptised. It was here that Lucia made her first communion, Francisco passed many hours in prayer, 'consoling the Hidden Jesus' and Jacinta had a vision of Our Lady, in which She taught her to meditate on the Rosary. On the right of the transept is the statue which Lucia refers to in her memoirs. The day is the eve of her First Communion, just after she had made her First Confession: 'In the church there was more than one statue of Our Lady; but as my sisters took care of the altar of Our Lady of the Rosary, I usually went there to pray. That is why I went there on this occasion also, to ask Her with all the ardour of my soul, to keep my poor heart for God alone. As I repeated this humble prayer over and over again, with my eyes fixed on the statue, it seemed to me that She smiled and, with a loving look and kindly gesture, assured me that She would. My heart was overflowing with joy, and I could scarcely utter a single word.'

In the cemetery adjacent to the Church on the south side, the bodies of Francisco and Jacinta lay before being transferred to the Basilica in the Sanctuary. Here also are buried many people prominent in the Fatima story, the children's parents, Canon Formigão etc.

The Rectory and the Services of the Sanctuary

In the area of the Rectory can be found the services for the benefit of pilgrims. Immediately on entering one finds the *Serviço de Pastoral Litúrgica (SEPALI)*, where all matters concerning the sacraments of baptism and matrimony are dealt with, as well as Mass intentions, subscriptions to the journal *Voz da Fátima*, and offerings.

Further into the building is the *Serviço de Peregrinos (SEPE)*, which helps private pilgrimages which want to organise their own activities or to participate in the activities of the sanctuary. Here also reservations for accommodation can be made in the houses which the Sanctuary manages, Our Lady of Sorrows, Our Lady of Carmel and the Paul VI Pastoral Centre *Serviço de Alojamentos (SEAL)*.

Everything concerning documentation, library, social records and the like is put in the hands of the *Serviço de Estudos e Difusão (SESDI)* which is also housed here, as is the Library.

The *Serviço de Doentes (SEDO)* (Service to the Infirm) and the *Secretariado do Movimento da Mensagem de Fátima*, (The Office for the Diffusion of the Message of Fatima) are situated behind the Chapel of the Apparitions.

THE FOLLOWING INFORMATION IS APPENDED HERE ONLY AS A MATTER OF INTEREST. IT IS A SERVICE NECESSARILY RESTRICTED TO THE PORTUGUESE PEOPLE.

Service to the Infirm (SEDO)
At present this service is only equipped to handle Portuguese pilgrims; space and facilities are stretched to the limit and many of the Portuguese

themselves must wait their turn. However, there is nothing to prevent the friends or relatives of any sick or invalided person from making their own arrangements for pilgrimage and applying to SEDO to be included in the formal Blessing of the Sick.

The Sanctuary of Fatima runs a hostel with various infirmaries equipped with those things necessary for the care of sick pilgrims. On the major pilgrimage days a medical corps and a team of nursing sisters are on hand to assist these pilgrims.

Because it is felt that Our Lady has a special concern for sick pilgrims the Sanctuary, since 1976, has promoted, through **SEDO**, retreats of three days for the sick and the physically handicapped, with accommodation offered not only for them but for those accompanying them. Annually there are 35 retreats with a total of 3,250 participants. Each retreat is in the care of at least one nurse, a doctor and two priests.

SEDO now functions under much improved conditions in the House of Our Lady of Sorrows. There is a monthly public bulletin entitled *Ponto de Encontro*. Information about the workings of this service may be had from: Servico de Doentes, Santuário de Fatima, 2496-908 Fatima Codex. Telef. (249) 532122

Policy for the Participation of the Sick in the Pilgrimages on 12th and 13th of the summer months:

With an end to bettering the pastoral care of the sick,

75

according to the spirit of the message of Our Lady delivered in Fatima, you are asked to take notice of the following paragraphs:

1. The Sanctuary invites the sick who wish to be in Fatima on either 13th May or October, to participate in the Spiritual Retreat which precedes and accompanies the Pilgrimage, from 9th to 13th. This retreat is free, though each patient is asked to give what he or she can manage in a closed, anonymous evelope.
    Bookings must be made with the Diocesan Secretary of the Movement of the Message of Fatima in the respective diocese.

2. To those who are unable to participate in the Retreat the best possible care will be given in one of the following options:

    First Option: The sick make their own arrangements; they receive the necessary medical care and nursing, they have a place reserved in the celebrations, and they take their meals with the others when desired. Bookings can only be made by presenting a medical report stating the respective ailment.

    Second Option: The patient receives all the care and the accommodation as well, in two possible ways, depending on the ailment: either common accommodation in dormitories, or interned in hospital wards. Those of the sick receiving accommodation are required to present their cooking requests to SEDO before 10th of the previous month, accompanied by a medical report where it is known that the sickness absolutely requires accommodation. A reply will be sent before the end of the month. You must not leave your house without having received it because it may not be possible to accommodate you.

3. Each patient may only participate once each year in order that the facility be open to the greatest number. Furthermore this service will not be available to persons who simply turn up and ask for a place.

The Postulation Centre

In the *Rua de S. Pedro*, on the north side of the Sanctuary, is a house with a name plate on the gatepost SECRETARIADO DOS PASTORINHOS. Inside is the Vice-Postulation Centre for Francisco and Jacinta Marto. It is part of the mechanics surrounding the Church's tradition of honouring God in the special graces he has given to certain people by proclaiming these people Venerable, then Blessed, then Saints.

No angel is despatched to tell us of each soul's status in the next life. God leaves such things to the initiative of the faithful and the wisdom and workings of the Church. In Rome a Curia office, the Congregation for the Causes of the Saints (established by Sixtus V in 1588 but reconstructed by John Paul II in 1983) processes writings, eye-witness statements, claims for miraculous intercession etc. provided by those postulating (i.e. asking, supplicating) the Cause of a holy person who has died. Vice-postulators work from the home base of the subject whose Cause is being forwarded.

This Vice-Postulation Centre for the Cause of Francisco and Jacinta Marto in Fatima functions independently of the Sanctuary. The Sanctuary cares for, promotes and organises the activities of the Shrine.

The Postulation office is concerned with the beatification, now achieved, and the canonisation of the young seers who died in 1919 and 1920. Apart from all the work required by Rome, the staff at the Centre kept in constant touch with the thousands of the faithful who shared their belief by sending out a newsletter every three months. This newsletter was, indeed still is, printed in seven different languages and keeps readers abreast of events pertinent to the Cause of the Marto children.

For many years the team at the *Secretariado dos Pastorinhos*, under the direction of an Hungarian priest, Fr. Louis Kondor SVD, have worked towards this end with singular devotion. When they started they were given no encouragement at all from Rome. There they were told that the beatification of children who were not formally considerd martyrs was unprecedented. Children, however pious, could not reach the level of heroic sanctity that distinguished a saint. Dominic Savio had been the candidate closest to being an exception and he had been under the constant guidance of a saint, Don Bosco, and had his short life catalogued by that saint's own hand. And Dominic Savio was fifteen. Here were two peasant children who hadn't even received the sacraments until they were at death's door at the age of ten. How could they expect a formal declaration of sanctity when great preachers, miracle workers and cloistered mystics were still undergoing the scrutiny of the Congregation for the Causes of the Saints?

But the vice-postulators at Rua de S. Pedro

reasoned that if children could be prodigies in music and the secular sciences why not in sanctity, and calmly went about their chosen task. Their persistent, unassuming work, fuelled by prayer has, as all the world now knows, been vindicated in the beatification of Francisco and Jacinta by Pope John Paul II in Fatima itself in May 2000.

The Centre has an hour-long film which it screens to parties of 8–140 pilgrims on request in its small cinema above the ground-floor offices.

In the basement of the building Fr. Kondor and his staff have assembled a visual treat for devotees of the Fatima story. It is a photographic reconstruction of the history of Fatima from 1917, full of seldom reproduced shots of the places, events and characters which fill the Fatima stage. The exhibits are divided into four sections:

The first section presents – to quote the brochure – *Aljustrel and the Parish of Fatima, with the seers and their families; The Apparitions of the Angel and of Our Lady; the illness, death and burial of the little shepherds, and the translation of their mortal remains to the Basilica. Then the life of the seer Lucia in Portugal and Spain is portrayed, her visit to Fatima in 1946 and her entrance into Carmel at Coimbra.*

Here are some beguiling presentations for the enthusiast, Francisco's signature, photos of people such as Artur de Oliveira Santos, called 'the Tinker', the Administrator of Ourem who kidnapped the children during the time appointed for the August apparitions. (He looks like a cross between Gary

Cooper and Humphrey Bogart; close inspection suggests that he is wearing a monocle over his right eye). And the kindly Mother Godinho who ran the orphanage in Lisbon's Estrela district which gave Jacinta shelter when no one else would accept her during the weeks before she went into the Estafânia Hospital for her operation – and death.

The second section shows *the development of the sanctuary from the construction of the little Chapel of the Apparitions.*

Here, among other things, we have a rare photo of Gilberto dos Anjos, the young man from Torres Novas who had a statue made to grace the new chapel, a statue which has since become one of the world's most familiar Marian images.

In this section, too, can be found twelve oil paintings by Sister Maria da Conceição, a nun of the Carmel of *S. José* in Fatima, according to Sister Lucia's directions and subsequently corrected by her in various details. These paintings depict the Three Apparitions of the Angel, the six Apparitions of Our Lady and the October visions showing St Joseph with the Infant on one side of the sun and Our Lady on the other, Our Lord, and Our Lady of Carmel.

The third section *presents the attitude of the Church towards Fatima, notably that of Popes Pius XII, Paul VI and JohnPaul II.*

Here we have Paul VI presenting Sister Lucia to the pilgrims in Fatima in 1967 and John Paul II with her in May 1982. Photographs showing the Way of the Cross and of the Hungarian Calvary are also in this section.

The fourth section houses slides and sound apparatus along with documents, books, stamps and objects used by the seers.

The postal address is Apartardo 6, 2496–908 Fatima. The telephone number is 249 532214 and office hours are:

Mon–Fri   9–12.30   2–5.30   Sat 9–12.30

Lafayette

Gift Monstrance to Fatima.

Designed and Manufactured
by
Gunning and Son Ltd. Dublin.

The Irish Monstrance, having been used for the blessing of the sick, on the Recinto Altar during the communions of the Mass, 13 October 1999.

The Basilica and Colonnades

Inside the Capelinha

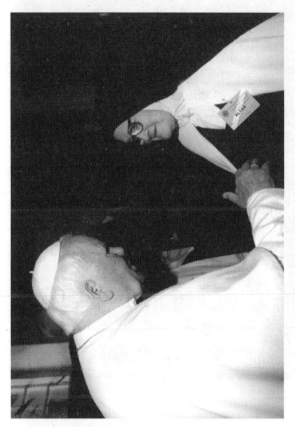

Sister Lucia and the Holy Father, May 2000

On special occasions First Communions are held at the
Cabeço site where the Angel appeared to the children. The
priest here is Fr Kondor, SVD of the Postulation Centre.
The recipient is José Lasota.

The Basilica and Recinto altar, on the night before the
May 2000 beatifications. Note the flags of the
Vatican and of Portugal.

The Statue in procession after a Sunday Mass.

The Holy Father places the ring given to him by Cardinal
Wyszynski at the feet of Our Lady's statue, 12 May 2000.

Candlelit Procession in Recinto

Official Programme for the Sanctuary

FROM EASTER TILL OCTOBER

Holy Week

Palm Sunday:

10.15: Blessing of the Palms and Procession.
11.00: Mass in the Recinto.
14.00: Stations of the Cross in the Recinto.
17.30: Sung Vespers in the Basilica.

Holy Thursday:

09.00: Sung Lauds in the Basilica.
14.30: Video in the Projection room. (In Portuguese.)
17.30: Solemn celebration of the Liturgy of the Supper of the Lord in the Basilica.
23.00: Communal prayer in the Basilica: the Agony of Jesus. (In Portuguese.)

Good Friday:

00.00–03.00: On foot to Valinhos, following the

sufferings of Our Lord on the night of His Passion.

09.00: Sung Lauds in the Basilica.
15.00: Celebration of the Death of Our Lord, in the Basilica.
21.00: Stations of the Cross in the Colonnade.

Holy Saturday:

09.00: Sung Lauds in the Basilica.
10.30: Video in the projection room. (In Portuguese.)
12.00: Rosary in the Capelinha.
15.00: Prayer to Our Lady of Sorrows in the Capelinha.
17.30: Sung vespers in the Basilica.

The Pascal Vigil:

22.00: The Liturgy of Light, of the Word, of Baptism and of the Eucharist, with the solemn celebration of the Pasch, in the Basilica. After the Liturgy, a Procession of the Most Holy Sacrament to the Chapel of Perpetual Adoration.

Easter Sunday:

Programme as for a normal Sunday.

Sundays and Holy Days of Obligation:

Saturday Evening:

15.00:   Sunday Mass in the Basilica.
16.30:   Sunday Mass in the Basilica.
17.00:   Procession to the Capelinha & Farewell to Our Lady.
18.30:   Sunday Mass in the Basilica.
21.30:   Rosary and Candlelight Procession. Capelinha.

Sundays (and Holy Days and National Holidays):

07.30:   Mass in the Basilica.
09.00:   Mass in the Basilica.
10.15:   Rosary in the Capelinha.
11.00:   International Mass at the altar of the Recinto, followed by the Farewell Procession.
12.30:   Mass in the Basilica.
14.00:   Prayer of Reparation to the Immaculate Heart of Mary in the Capelinha.
15.00:   Mass in the Basilica.
16.00:   Rosary in the Capelinha.
16.30:   Mass in the Basilica.
17.30:   Eucharistic Procession in the Recinto.
18.30:   Mass in the Basilica.
21.30:   Rosary and Candlelight Procession in the Capelinha.

Weekdays (from Monday to Saturday morning):

07.30: Mass in the Basilica.
09.00: Mass in the Basilica (Thursdays in the Capelinha).
11.00: Mass in the Basilica.
12.00: Rosary in the Capelinha.
12.30: Mass in the Capelinha.
14.00: Prayer of Reparation to the Immaculate Heart of Mary in the Capelinha.
15.00: Mass in the Basilica.
16.30: Mass in the Basilica.
18.30: Mass in the Basilica.
Rosary in the Capelinha – radio broadcast.
21.30: Rosary in the Capelinha, followed by Candlelight Procession.

First Thursday:

21.30: After the Rosary – Prayer for priests with exposition and procession of the Most Blessed Sacrament.

First Friday:

21.30: After the Rosary – Prayer of Reparation to the Most Sacred Heart of Jesus in the Capelinha.

First Saturday:

Pilgrims are advised to check the official programme for this devotion, specially requested by Our Lady during the Apparitions.

21.30:   Rosary in the Capelinha – radio broadcast.

12TH AND 13TH OF EACH MONTH FROM MAY TO OCTOBER

12th Morning:

07.30:   Mass in the Basilica.
08.30:   The Stations of the Cross to Valinhos.
09.00:   Mass in the Basilica.
11.00:   Mass in the Basilica.
12.30:   Mass in the Basilica.

Masses in the Capelinha:

07.30:   in German.
08.30:   in English.
09.30:   in French.
10.30:   in Spanish.
11.30:   in Dutch.
12.30:   in Italian.
13.30:   in Polish. (Or other languages.)

12th Afternoon:

16.30: Mass for the sick in the north colonnade, followed by a Procession of the Most Holy Sacrament.

18.30: Official opening of the pilgrimage in the Capelinha.

21.30: Solemn blessing of the candles and Rosary in the Capelinha followed by the Candlelight Procession.

22.30: International Mass at the Precinct Altar.

13th Night Vigil:

0000–0200: Adoration of the Most Holy Sacrament.

0200–0330: Stations of the Cross.

0330–0430: Marian Celebration.

0430–0530: Mass.

0530–0700: Adoration of the Most Holy Sacrament with Lauds.

07.00: Procession of the Most Holy Sacrament.

13th Morning (Final celebration):

09.15: Rosary in the Capelinha.

10.00: Procession, Mass, Benediction of the Sick, Consecration and Farewell.

9TH–10TH JUNE: THE CHILDREN'S PILGRIMAGE

(This is a Portuguese custom and is only timetabled here as a matter of interest.)

9th June:

During the day the normal programme of the Sanctuary is followed:
21.30:   Marian celebration.

10th June:

09.30:   Events staged in the Paul VI Centre.
11.30:   Mass in the Recinto.
15.00:   Events staged in the Paul VI Centre for the children who did not participate in the morning.
15.45:   Rosary, Consecration and Farewell in the Capelinha.

15TH JULY – 15TH SEPTEMBER: THE PROGRAMME FOR ONE DAY PILGRIMAGES
(Except for the 12th and 13th of the months, Sundays, Holy Days and National Holidays.)

(This is a Portuguese custom and is only timetabled here as a matter of interest.)

From Monday to Friday:

10.15: Greeting Our Lady in the Capelinha.
10.30: A guided tour of the Sanctuary – the Basilica, The Chapel of St Joseph, the Colonnade, the Chapel of Perpetual Adoration.
12.00: Rosary, in the Capelinha.
12.30: Mass in the Capelinha.
15.00: Video: *Fatima, An Experience of Faith.*
16.00: By bus to visit Valinhos, the Hungarian Calvary and the Chapel of St Stephen, the Place of the Angel, the houses of the Little Shepherds and the Museum of Aljustrel.
18.00: Return to the Sanctuary, with onward transport to the Bus Terminal if necessary.

Saturday:

10.15: Greeting Our Lady in the Chapel of the Apparitions.
10.25: Film: *Apparition.*
12.00: Rosary in the Capelinha.
12.30: Mass in the Capelinha.
16.00: The Stations of the Cross on foot, with a visit to Valinhos, the Place of the Angel and the houses of the Little Shepherds. Prayer in the Chapel of St Stephen.
19.00: Anticipated hour of return, by foot.

THE MONTH OF AUGUST: ADORATION OF THE BLESSED SACRAMENT

(From Monday to Friday except on 12th, 13th and 15th.)

The following programme is organised as a response to the invitation of the angel at Loca do Cabeço:

15.00: International Mass in the Basilica.

16.00: Silent Adoration in the Basilica.

17.30: Eucharistic Procession to the Chapel of Perpetual Adoration and Benediction of the Most Holy Sacrament.

Note: There is a Mass at 16.30 in the Capelinha.

14TH AND 15TH AUGUST: THE ASSUMPTION OF THE BLESSED VIRGIN MARY

14th – The Vigil of the Assumption:

21.30: Rosary in the Capelinha followed by a Candle Procession to the Recinto altar.

22.30: Solemn chanting of the hymn *Akathistos*[1].

[1] Or *Acathistus*. It is a Byzantine hymn, almost an office when sung in its entirety, in honour of the Mother of God. The Greek word means 'not sitting' as it was originally sung standing, perhaps all night. Booklets with the words of the *Akathistos* in English, and other languages, are freely available.

91

Then a return to the Capelinha singing the *Ladainha Laurentana*[2] in Latin.

23.30: Hymns to Our Lady, in different languages, in the Capelinha. (Prior arrangements can be made with SEPE.)

24.00: Conclusion of the vigil.

15th – The Feast of the Assumption:

08.15: Sung Lauds in the Capelinha.

10.15: Rosary in the Capelinha followed by the Liturgical Procession to the *Recinto* Altar.

11.00: International Mass at the *Recinto* Altar.

14.00: Prayer of Reparation to Our Lady by the Religious Communities of Cova da Iria in the Capelinha.

16.00: 'Young People Praise Our Lady' in the Capelinha.

17.30: Eucharistic Procession in the *Recinto*.

21.00: Rosary in the Capelinha and the Candle Procession.

19th – Anniversary of the Fourth Apparition of Our Lady:

09.00: International Mass in the Capelinha.

21.30: A Procession from the Capelinha to Valinhos, reciting the Rosary. Adoration and Prostration at Loca do Cabeço.

---

[2] The Litany of Loreto.

NATIONAL HOLIDAYS

25th April, 1st May, 5th October

10.15:   Rosary in the Capelinha.
11.00:   International Mass in the Capelinha or at the Recinto Altar, followed by a Procession of Farewell.
17.30:   A Eucharistic Procession in the Recinto.

FEASTS OF OUR LADY

09.00:   International Mass in the Capelinha.
31st May – The Visitation. (Closes May celebrations.)
16th July – Our Lady of Carmel.
8th Sept. – Nativity of Our Lady.
15th Sept. – Our Lady of Sorrows.
7th Oct. – Our Lady of the Rosary.

THERE IS A MASS IN ENGLISH EACH WEEKDAY FROM JULY TO SEPTEMBER AT 1530HRS AT THE CAPELINHA.

There are confessions daily in the *Capela da Reconciliação* beneath the east colonnade. From 07.30 to 13.00 and from 14.00 to 19.30.

There is a free video showing, in English, of a dramatised version of the Fatima story at 12.00 each day during the summer months. The video theatre is on your right as you leave the main concourse through the exit beneath the north colonnade, directly in front of the great holm-oak. Just walk in.

Mass times, regular and unscheduled, for both the Basilica and the Capelinha are posted around 19.00 hrs each evening of the year for the following day in four locations:

1. On the Informações notice board behind the candle pyre.
2. On the south-western side of the Capelinha.
3. On the north-eastern side of the Capelinha.
4. In the Basilica foyer.

FROM NOVEMBER TO EASTER
Sundays and Holy Days

Saturday afternoon:

15.00:   The Sunday Mass in the Basilica.
16.30:   The Sunday Mass in the Basilica.
18.30:   The Sunday Mass in the Basilica.
21.00:   Rosary in the Capelinha or the Basilica.

Sundays, Holy Days and National Holidays:

07.30:   Mass in the Basilica.
09.00:   Mass in the Basilica.
10.15:   Rosary in the Capelinha.
11.00:   International Mass in the Capelinha or Basilica.

12.30: Mass in the Basilica.
14.00: Prayer of Reparation to the Immaculate
        Conception in the Capelinha.
15.00: Mass in the Basilica.
16.00: Rosary in the Capelinha.
16.30: Mass in the Basilica.
17.30: Sung Vespers in the Basilica.
18.30: Mass in the Basilica.

Weekdays –
From Monday to Saturday Morning:

07.30: Mass in the Basilica.
09.00: Mass in the Basilica.
11.00: Mass in the Basilica.
12.00: Rosary in the Capelinha.
12.30: Mass in the Capelinha.
15.00: Mass in the Basilica.
16.30: Mass in the Basilica.
18.30: Mass in the Basilica.
        Rosary in the Capelinha – broadcast.
21.00: Rosary and Candlelit Procession. (But only
        on the initiative of private groups, and not
        during Lent.)

First Thursdays:

19.00: After the broadcast Rosary – Prayer for
        priests, with exposition of the Blessed
        Sacrament in the Capelinha.

First Fridays:

19.00:   After the broadcast Rosary – Prayer of
          Reparation to the Sacred heart of Jesus in
          the Capelinha.

First Saturday:

          Pilgrims are advised to check the official
          programme for this devotion which was
          especially requested by Our Lady during the
          apparitions.

21.00:   Rosary in the Capelinha – broadcast.

THE 12TH AND 13TH MONTHLY PILGRIMAGE FROM NOV. TO APRIL:

12th:

21.00:   Rosary and Candlelight Procession in the
          Capelinha.

13th:

10.15:   Rosary in the Capelinha.
11.00:   Mass, in the Capelinha or the Basilica.

1st December, National Holiday:

Programme as for Sundays and Holy Days.

7th and 8th December:
(The Immaculate Conception)

7th:

21.00: Rosary in the Capelinha, and the Candlelight Procession to the Basilica followed by the singing of the hymn *Akathistos*.

8th:

10.15: Rosary in the Capelinha.
11.00: Solemn Mass in the Capelinha.

24th and 25th December:
(Christmas – Holy Day)

24th The Christmas Vigil:

23.00: Rehearsal & Office of the lessons in the Basilica.

25th Solemnity of the Nativity of the Lord:

00.00: Mass in the Basilica. Kissing of the Infant.
17.30: Sung vespers in the Basilica.

Sunday after Christmas – Feast of the Holy Family:

10.15: Rosary in the Capelinha.
11.00: Mass, with Consecration of Families, in the Capelinha.

31st December:

22.00: Mass followed by *Te Deum*.
22.30: Tea and cakes in the Retreat House (Nª Sª dos Dores) to celebrate the New Year.

1st January – Holy Mary Mother of God. Day of World Peace. Anniversary of the Perpetual Adoration:

00.15: Rosary to ask for blessing for the New Year, in the Capelinha.
15.00: Mass in the Capelinha followed by Procession of the Most Holy Sacrament to the Chapel of Perpetual Adoration.

Shrove Tuesday:

Programme as on 1st December.

2nd February – Feast of the Presentation:

17.30:   Rosary in the Capelinha.
18.00:   Blessing of the candles and liturgical procession to Mass in the Basilica, with the renewal of vows.

Lent – The Stations of the Cross:
The First Sunday:

14.00–1800 – From Olivais to the Sanctuary on foot (12Km).

Sundays II III IV & V:

14.00:   in the Recinto.

Fridays:

14.00:   in the Colonnade (the columns in front of the Basilica.)

MASS OF OUR LADY OF FATIMA

ENTRANCE ANTIPHON

Hebr. 4:16

Let us have no fear in approaching the throne of grace to receive mercy (Alleluia).

Celebrant: The Grace of Our Lord Jesus Christ and the love of God and the fellowship of the Holy Spirit be with you all.

People: And also with you.

PENITENTIAL RITE

C: My brothers and sisters,
to prepare ourselves to celebrate the sacred mysteries, let us call to mind our sins.

All: I confess to Almighty God,
and to you, my brothers and sisters,
that I have sinned through my own fault,
in my thoughts and in my words,
in what I have done,
and in what I have failed to do;
and I ask the blessed Mary, ever virgin,
all the angels and saints,
and you, my brothers and sisters,
to pray for me to the Lord our God.

C: May Almighty God have mercy on us,
forgive us our sins,
and bring us to everlasting life.

P: Amen.

THE KYRIE

C: Lord, have mercy.
P: Lord, have mercy.
C: Christ, have mercy.
P: Christ, have mercy.
C: Lord, have mercy.
P: Christ, have mercy.

THE GLORIA

All: Glory to God in the highest,
And peace to his people on earth.

Lord God, heavenly King,
almighty God and Father,
we worship you, we give you thanks,
we praise you for your glory.

Lord Jesus Christ, only Son of the Father,
Lord God, Lamb of God,
you take away the sins of the world:
have mercy on us;

you are seated at the right hand of the Father,
receive our prayer.

For you alone are the Holy One,
you alone are the Lord,
you alone are the Most High,
Jesus Christ,
with the Holy Spirit,
in the glory of God the Father. Amen.

OPENING PRAYER

C: Let us pray.
Father,
you have given us the mother of your Son
to be our mother also.
Grant us that,
by obeying the appeals of the Blessed Virgin Mary,
we may always work through prayer and penance
for the kingdom of Christ
and attain eternal happiness.
We ask this through Our Lord Jesus Christ your Son,
who lives and reigns with you and the Holy Spirit,
one God, for ever and ever.
P: Amen.

THE LITURGY OF THE WORD

Reading   **Apoc. 21: 1–5a**

**I saw the new Jerusalem,
As beautiful as a bride all dressed for her husband.**

A reading from the book of the Apocalypse:

I, John, saw a new heaven and a new earth;
the first heaven and the first earth
had disappeared now,
and there was no longer any sea.
I saw the holy city, and the new Jerusalem,
coming down from God out of heaven,
as beautiful as a bride all dressed for her husband.
Then I heard a loud voice call from the throne,
'You see this city?
Here God lives among men.
He will make his home among them;
they shall be his people,
and he will be their God;
his name is God-with-them.
He will wipe away all tears from their eyes;
There will be no more death,
and no more mourning or sadness.
The world of the past has gone.'
Then the One sitting on the throne spoke:
'Now I am making the whole of creation new.'

This is the Word of the Lord.
P: Thanks be to God.

RESPONSORIAL PSALM
JUDITH 13: 18–20

R. You are the highest honour of our race.

May you be blessed, my daughter,
By God Most High, beyond all women on earth;
And may the Lord God be blessed,
The Creator of heaven and earth. **R**.

The trust you have shown
Shall not pass from the memories of men,
But shall ever remind them of the power of God. **R**.

God grant you always be held in honour,
And rewarded with blessings,
Since you did not consider your own life
When our nation was brought to its knees. **R**.

ALLELUIA   LUKE 1: 45

R. Alleluia, alleluia.

V. Blessed are you Virgin Mary,
Who believed that the promise made you
By the Lord would be fulfilled. **R**.

GOSPEL

C: The Lord be with you.
P: And also with you.

JOHN 19: 25–27

C: ✠ A reading from the Holy Gospel according to John
P: Glory to you, Lord.

Near the cross of Jesus stood his mother
And his mother's sister,
Mary the wife of Clopas, and Mary of Magdala.
Seeing his mother
and the disciple he loved standing near her,
Jesus said to his mother,
'Woman, this is your son.'
Then to the disciple he said,
'This is your mother.'
And from that moment
The disciple made a place for her in his home.

This is the Gospel of the Lord.

THE CREED

We believe in one God,
the Father, the Almighty,
maker of heaven and earth,
of all that is, seen and unseen.

We believe in one Lord, Jesus Christ,
the only Son of God,
eternally begotten of the Father,
God from God, Light from Light,
true God from true God,
begotten, not made,
of one Being with the Father.
Through him all things were made.
For us men and for our salvation
he came down from heaven:
by the power of the Holy Spirit
he became incarnate from the Virgin Mary
and was made man.
For our sake he was crucified under Pontius Pilate;
he suffered death and was buried.
On the third day he rose again
in accordance with the Scriptures;
he ascended into heaven
and is seated at the right hand of the Father.
He will come again in glory to judge
the living and the dead,
and his kingdom will have no end.

We believe in the Holy Spirit,
the Lord, the giver of life,
who proceeds from the Father and the Son.
With the Father and the Son
he is worshipped and glorified.
He has spoken through the prophets.
We believe in one holy catholic and apostolic Church.
We acknowledge one baptism
for the forgiveness of sins.
We look for the resurrection of the dead,
and the life of the world to come. Amen.

PRAYER OF THE FAITHFUL

Here, at this Sacred spot,
Where the Most Holy Virgin Mary appeared,
Let us present our prayers to God our Father,
Who gave us the Mother of his Son to be our Mother.

(The following prayers might be replaced by others.)

1. For all the faithful,
     that by obeying the appeals of Mary
     in a spirit of true penance and prayer,
     they may work wholeheartedly
     for the renewal of the world
     and for the Kingdom of Christ,
     we pray to the Lord.

2. For those who exercise sacred ministry
   in the Church,
   that they may be attentive to the word of God,
   love it and proclaim it with fidelity and
   enthusiasm,
   as Mary did,
   we pray to the Lord.

3. For those who govern nations,
   that they may work for justice and peace
   in the world,
   and harmoniously collaborate
   in the just distribution
   of earthly goods among all the inhabitants
   of the world,
   we pray to the Lord.

4. For all those who suffer,
   that in union with Mary, consoler of the afflicted,
   in the loving care of others
   and in the contemplation of the Cross of Christ,
   they may find courage to face life,
   we pray to the Lord.

5. For all of us here present and for our families
   (for our nation ... for our city ...)
   that by the intercession of Mary,
   those who seek Christ may find Him,
   sinners may be converted,
   young people may open their hearts
   with enthusiasm to the Gospel,
   we pray to the Lord.

God of infinite goodness,
attentive to the supplication of your people,
and with the prayers of Mary,
Mother of your Son and Mother of the Church,
to help us, listen to our pleas and increase our faith.
We ask this through Jesus Christ your Son
in the unity of the Holy Spirit.

P: Amen.

THE LITURGY OF THE EUCHARIST

C: Blessed are you, Lord, God of all creation.
Through your goodness we have this bread to offer,
which earth has given and human hands have made.
It will become for us the bread of life.

P: Blessed be God forever.

C: By the mystery of this water and wine
may we come to share in the divinity of Christ,
who humbled himself to share in our humanity.
Blessed are you, Lord, God of all creation.
Through your goodness we have this wine to offer,
fruit of the vine and work of human hands.
It will become our spiritual drink.

P: Blessed be God forever.

C: Lord God, we ask you to receive us
and be pleased with the sacrifice we offer you
with humble and contrite hearts.

Lord, wash away my iniquity; cleanse me from my
sin.

Pray, brethren, that our sacrifice
may be acceptable to God the almighty Father.

P: May the Lord accept the sacrifice at your hands
for the praise and glory of his name,
for our good, and the good of all his Church.

PRAYER OVER THE GIFTS

Lord, we offer these gifts of reparation and of praise
so that in celebrating the feast of the
Blessed Virgin Mary,
you may absolve us from our sins
and guide our wavering hearts.
We ask this in the name of Jesus the Lord.

P: Amen.

PREFACE

C: The Lord be with you.
P: And also with you.
C: Lift up your hearts.
P: We lift them up to the Lord.

C: Let us give thanks to the Lord our God.
P: It is right to give him thanks and praise.

Father, all-powerful and ever-living God,
we do well always and everywhere
to give you thanks,
as we celebrate the feast of the Blessed Virgin Mary
and praise you for your gifts.

She, receiving your Word in her Immaculate Heart,
merited to conceive him in her virginal womb,
and in giving birth to the Creator of the world,
she prepared the birth of the Church.

She, in receiving at the foot of the cross
the testament of divine charity,
received all men as her children,
born to eternal life through the death of Christ.

She, when the apostles were awaiting
the coming of the Holy Spirit, the promised one,
united her supplications
to the prayers of the disciples,
and thus became the model of the supplicant Church.

111

She, then finally elevated to the glory of heaven,
surrounds with her maternal love the pilgrim Church
and lovingly directs their steps
to the heavenly dwelling place,
until the glorious coming of the Lord.

And so, with all the angels and saints
we proclaim your glory
and join in their unending hymn of praise.

All: Holy, holy, holy Lord, God of power and might,
       heaven and earth are full of your glory.
           Hosanna in the highest.
  Blessed is he who comes in the name of the Lord.
           Hosanna in the highest.

EUCHARISTIC PRAYER

C: Father, you are holy indeed,
And all creation rightly gives you praise.
All life, all holiness comes from you
Through your Son, Jesus Christ our Lord,
By the working of the Holy Spirit.
From age to age you gather a people to yourself,
So that from east to west
A perfect offering may be made
To the glory of your name.

And so, Father, we bring you these gifts.
We ask you to make them holy
by the power of your Spirit,
That they may become the body and blood
Of your son, our Lord Jesus Christ,
At whose command we celebrate this Eucharist.

On the night he was betrayed,
he took bread and gave you thanks and praise.
He broke the bread, gave it to his disciples, and said:

> *Take this, all of you, and eat it:*
> *this is my body*
> *which will be given up for you.*

When supper was ended, he took the cup.
Again he gave you thanks and praise,
gave the cup to his disciples, and said:

> *Take this, all of you, and drink from it:*
> *this is the cup of my blood,*
> *the blood of the new and everlasting covenant.*
> *It will be shed for you and for all men*
> *so that sins may be forgiven.*
> *Do this in memory of me.*

Let us proclaim the mystery of faith:
Dying you destroyed our death,
Rising you restored our life.
Lord Jesus, come in glory.

Father, calling to mind
the death your Son endured for our salvation,
his glorious resurrection and ascension into heaven,
and ready to greet him when he comes again,
we offer you in thanksgiving
this holy and living sacrifice.

Look with favour on your Church's offering,
And see the victim
whose death has reconciled us to yourself.
Grant that we,
who are nourished by his body and blood,
may be filled with his Holy Spirit,
and become one body, one spirit in Christ.

May he make us an everlasting gift to you
And enable us to share in the inheritance of your saints,
With Mary, the virgin Mother of God;
With the apostles, the martyrs,
Saint (N...) and all your saints
On whose constant intercession we rely for help.

Lord, may this sacrifice,
Which has made our peace with you,
Advance the peace and salvation of all the world.
Strengthen in faith and love
your pilgrim Church on earth;
Your servant Pope John Paul, our bishop Seraphim,
And all the bishops,
With the clergy and the entire people
your son has gained for you.

Father hear the prayers of the family
you have gathered here before you.
In mercy and love unite all your children
Wherever they may be.
Welcome into your kingdom
our departed brothers and sisters,
and all who have left this world
in your friendship.
We hope to enjoy forever
The vision of your glory,
Through Christ our Lord
through whom all good things come.

THROUGH HIM,
WITH HIM,
IN HIM,
IN THE UNITY OF THE HOLY SPIRIT,
ALL GLORY AND HONOUR IS YOURS,
ALMIGHTY FATHER,
FOR EVER AND EVER.
P: Amen.

RITE OF COMMUNION

C: Let us pray with confidence to the Father
in the words our Saviour gave us:

All: Our Father, who art in heaven,
Hallowed be thy name;
Thy Kingdom come;

Thy will be done on earth as it is in heaven.
Give us this day our daily bread;
and forgive us our trespasses
as we forgive those who trespass against us;
and lead us not into temptation,
but deliver us from evil.

C: Deliver us, Lord, from every evil,
and grant us peace in our day.
In your mercy keep up free from sin
and protect us from all anxiety
as we wait in joyful hope
for the coming of our Saviour, Jesus Christ.

All: For the kingdom, the power,
and the glory are yours, now and forever.

C: Lord Jesus Christ, you said to your apostles:
I leave you peace, my peace I give you.
Look not on our sins, but the faith of your Church,
and grant us the peace and unity of your kingdom
where you live for ever and ever.
P: Amen.

C: Let us offer each other the sign of peace.

All: Lamb of God, you take away the sins of the world:
have mercy on us.
Lamb of God, you take away the sins of the world:
have mercy on us.
Lamb of God, you take away the sins of the world:
grant us peace.

116

C: May this mingling of the body and blood
of our Lord Jesus Christ
bring eternal life to those who receive it.
Lord Jesus Christ,
with faith in your love and mercy
I eat your body and drink your blood.
Let it not bring me condemnation,
but health in mind and body.

This is the Lamb of God
who takes away the sins of the world.
Happy are those who are called to his supper.

All: Lord, I am not worthy to receive you,
but only say the word and I shall be healed.

COMMUNION ANTIPHON

JUDITH 13: **24–25**

Blessed be the Lord God,
Who gave such great honour to your name:
All generations will sing your praises. (Alleluia)

C: The body of Christ.
The blood of Christ.

PRAYER AFTER COMMUNION

Lord, having received with joy
these heavenly sacraments,
grant us, we pray you,
that they may lead us to eternal life
where we may rejoice forever
with the Blessed Virgin Mary,
Mother of your Son and Mother of the Church.
We ask this through Christ our Lord.

C: The Lord be with you.
P: And also with you.

       C: May almighty God bless you,
             The Father,
             And the Son,

             ✠

       and the Holy Spirit.
         P: Amen.

Hymns

The most popular hymn in Fatima is the *Ave de Fatima*, even the Basilica bells ring it out on the hour, every hour.

Below we give the original Portuguese words if you feel you want to join in a verse or two after a Portuguese Mass in the Capelinha. We also provide a transliteration which might read awkwardly but follows the Portuguese as closely as possible.

Then there are five verses of the translation usually sung by Irish or English pilgrims, and seven verses of the version sung by the Blue Army at the Shrine of the Immaculate Heart in Washington, New Jersey, USA.

The refrain **AVE, AVE, AVE MARIA!** is sung twice after each verse.

AVE DE FATIMA

1	A treze de Maio, Na Cova da Iria, Apareceu brilhando A Virgem Maria.	On the thirteenth of May in the Cova da Iria The Virgin Mary appeared shining.

2   A Virgem Maria,
    Cercada de luz,
    Nossa Mãe bendita
    E Mãe de Jesus.

    The Virgin Mary
    surrounded by light
    Our Blessed Mother and
    the Mother of Jesus.

3   Foi aos Pastorinhos
    Que a Virgem falou.
    Desde então nas almas
    Nova luz brilhou.

    It was to the little
    shepherds that the Virgin
    spoke. Since then a new
    light has shone in souls.

4   Com doces palavras
    Mandou-nos rezar
    A Virgem Maria
    Para nos salvar.

    With sweet words the
    Virgin Mary told us to
    pray for our salvation.

5   Mas jamais esqueçam
    Nossos corações
    Que nos fez a Virgem
    Determinações.

    But our hearts ever forget
    the resolutions we make
    to the Virgin.

6   Falou contra o luxo,
    Contra o impudor
    De imodestas modas
    De uso pecador

    She spoke against lust,
    against impurity, of the
    immodest clothes that
    sinners wear.

7   Disse que a pureza
    Agrada a Jesus,
    Disse que a luxúria
    Ao fogo conduz.

    She said that purity was
    pleasing to Jesus, She said
    that lust leads to the fire.

8   A treze de Outubro   On the thirteenth of
Foi o seu adeus   October is was Her farewell
E a Virgem Maria   and the Virgin Mary
Voltou para os céus   returned to heaven.

9   À Pátria que é vossa,   To our country, which is
Senhora dos Céus,   yours, heavenly lady, give
Dai honra, alegria   honour, joy and the grace
E a graça de Deus   of God.

10   À Virgem bendita   Let all our land sing the
Cante seu louvor   praises of the Blessed
Toda a nossa terra   Virgin in a hymn of love.
Num hino de amor.

11   Todo o mundo a louve All the world praises to
Para se salvar,   save itself – from the valley
Desde o vale ao monte, to the mountain, from the
Desde o monte ao mar. mountain to the sea.

12   Ah! dêmos-Lhe graças Ah, we give thanks to Her
Por nos dar seu bem,   for the good She does
À Virgem Maria,   us, to the Virgin Mary,
Nossa querida Mãe!   our dear Mother.

13   E para pagarmos   And to pay for so much
Tal graça e favor,   grace and favour, our souls
Tenham nossas almas only have good will and
Só bondade e amor   love.

14 Ave, Virgem Santa,
    'strela que nos guia!
    Ave, Mãe de Igreja
    Oh! Virgem Maria!

Hail, Holy Virgin, star
which guides us! Hail,
Mother of the Church,
Oh Virgin Mary!

FATIMA AVE (European English)

1 The thirteenth of May
   In the Cova d'Iria
   Appeared, oh so brilliant,
   The Virgin Maria.

2 The Virgin Maria
   Encircled with light,
   Our own dearest Mother
   And heaven's delight.

3 To three little shepherds
   Our Lady appeared
   The light of Her grace
   To Her Son souls endeared.

4 With war and its evils
   The whole world was seething
   And countless of thousands
   Were mourning and weeping.

5 By honouring Mary
   And loving Her Son
   The peace of the world
   Will most surely be won.

FATIMA AVE (The American version)

1   In Fatima's Cove
    On the thirteenth of May
    The Virgin Maria
    Appeared at midday.

2   The Virgin Maria
    Surrounded by light
    God's mother is ours,
    For She gives us this sight.

3   The world was then suffering
    From war, plague and strife,
    And Portugal mourned
    For her great loss of life.

4   To three shepherd children
    The Virgin then spoke
    A message so hopeful
    With peace for all folk.

5   With sweet Mother's pleading
    She asked us to pray.
    Do penance, be modest,
    The Rosary each day.

6   All Portugal heard
    What God's Mother did say,
    Converted, it sings of
    That Queen to this day.

7   We all must remember
    Our Lady's request
    Do all that She asks for,
    Obey Her behests.

The hymns in Latin one might meet during devotions in the Sanctuary are The *Salve Regina* and the Benediction hymns. The texts of these follow.

SALVE REGINA

Salve Regina,
Mater misericordiae.
Vita, dulcedo et spes nostra, salve!
Ad Te clamamus, exules filii Hevae,
Ad te suspiramus, gementes et flentes
In hac lacrimarum valle.
Eia ergo, Advocata nostra,
Illos tuos misericordes oculos
Ad nos converte.
Et Jesum,
Benedictum fructum ventris tui
Nobis post hoc exilium ostende.
O clemens!
O pia!
O dulcis Virgo Maria.

The Benediction Hymns in Latin

Sadly Benediction of the Blessed Sacrament has fallen out of use in many parishes and religious houses throughout the world. In Fatima, however, it remains a very lively expression of the faith of pilgrims. On most days during the month of August there is a Eucharistic procession at 1700 from the Basilica around the south colonnade, terminating in Benediction of the Blessed Sacrament outside the Lausperene. For those of us who have forgotten, or never knew, the Latin hymns traditionally sung during Benediction, here are the words:

O SALUTARIS

O salutaris hóstia,
Quae caeli pandis óstium,
Bella premunt hostília,
Da robur, fer auxílium.

Uni trinóque Dómino
Sit sempitérna glória,
Qui vitam sine término
Nobis donet in pátria. Amen.

TANTUM ERGO

Tantum ergo Sacraméntum
Venerémur cérnui:
Et antíquum documentum
Novo cedat rítui;
Praestet fides suppleméntum
Sénsuum deféctui.

Genitóri, Genitóque
Laus et jubilátio,
Salus, honor, virtus quoque
Sit et benedíctio;
Procedénti ab utroque
Compar sit laudátio. Amen.

P: Panem de caelo preastitísti eis. (Alleluia.)
C: Omne delectaméntum in se habéntem. (Alleluia.)

OREMUS

Deus, qui nobis sub Sacraménto mirábili passiónis tuae memóriam reliquísti: tríbue, quáesumus, ita nos córporis et sánguinis tui sacra mystéria venerári, ut redemptiónis tuae fructum in nobis júgiter sentiámus. Qui vivis et regnis in saecula seculorum. Amen.

ADOREMUS

Adorémus in aetérnum Sanctíssimum Sacraméntum.

Laudáte Dóminum omnes gentes;
Laudáte eum omnes pópuli.
Quóniam confirmáta est super nos misericórdia ejus:
Et véritas Dómini manet in aetérnum.

Glória Patri, et Fílio, et Spirítui Sancto.
Sicut erat in princípio, et nunc, et semper,
et in sáecula saeculórum. Amen.

Adorémus in aetúrnum Sanctíssimum Sacraméntum.

The Chapel of Reconciliation
(A Capela da Reconciliação)
The Confessionals.

Though conversion of the heart is a secret only known to God, frequent use of the Sacrament of Reconciliation, (or Penance, or Confession) is an indication of an individual's desire to be involved in those things which pertain to Him. Fatima has always had a very strong appeal for conciliation, or reconciliation, of man with God and for this reason the present *Capela da Reconciliação* was inaugurated in August 1992.

It is situated almost on the ground level beneath the south colonnade, between the Basilica and the Lausperene. Above its glass, iron-latticed doors is a sign in large green letters CAPELA DA RECONCILIAÇÃO and on a board beneath the word CONFESSIONS in four languages. The French, Italian and English, which use the Latin root, are all spelt pretty much the same. The German *Beichten* stands out.

Although this facility is called a chapel it is in fact a series of purpose built oratories with confessionals. Beyond the glass doors, entering from the precinct, you find yourself in a foyer. To the right seven steps lead down to those confessionals in which the Portuguese language is the usual medium of communication.

128

The Portuguese Confessionals

Immediately below the seven steps is an oratory with benches on either side of a central aisle, the right benches facing a large graphic crucifix, the left facing a statue of the Immaculate Heart. The aisle leads into another long oratory with benches on the right and ten confessionals in wood and smoked glass on the left. A green light on the upper jamb of each confessional indicates that a priest is on call inside. The name of the priest is usually displayed on a printed card. In the winter months languages other than Portuguese also spoken by the priest are written here. Inside each box you can confess either through a grille, kneeling, or sit on a chair facing the confessor.

Confessionals in Languages Other Than Portuguese

Back in the foyer a sign with an arrow pointing left announces confessions in French, Italian, German and English. Following this arrow you find yourself facing an oratory with five confessionals on the right. These have the languages used painted on the smoked glass outside, along with the green light system. If the confessor in any one of the confessionals speaks another language the extra language is advertised.

Running parallel with this oratory is another to the right. This has six confessionals, the one immediately to the right inside the door being specially constructed for use by disabled penitents. German speaking priests usually use this section, along with organised groups employing other languages.

If there is no English-speaking confessor in the English box there is always an usher on duty. This usher is usually one of the sisters from one of the local convents. Several speak English, but even if the one on duty when you are looking for a priest doesn't, the word 'English' is enough for her to direct you to the Portuguese confessionals where the priest on duty speaks English. If there isn't one on duty at that moment, then she will tell you what time the next one will be due. These sisters are invariably helpful and understanding. They are usually wearing a yellow armband with the words *Serviço do Santuário. Confisões* printed on them.

The opening hours of the Capela da Reconciliação are:

07.30–13.00
14.00–19.30
14.00–18.00 are the hours advertised for the English box but this depends very much on the availability of a native English speaking priest. But many of the Italian and Spanish priests there speak excellent English.

NB: Confessions on 12th and 13th of the summer months are in the Paul VI Pastoral Centre but these are for Portuguese pilgrims.

12th: 09.00–24.00
13th: 06.00–11.00

Facts and statistics

During the first full year of the Capela da Reconciliação opening (1st Jan.–31st Dec. 1993) 117,138 people approached the sacrament here of whom 70% were women and 30% men. When it is considered that not all the penitents were registered and that this number doesn't include the anniversary pilgrimages of the summer, nor all those who confess in the religious houses of Fatima, 150,000 pilgrims approaching the Sacrament might be a fair estimate. That was 1992 and each year since has seen an increase in absolutions.

Before 1992 confessions were heard behind the fourteen altars of the side chapels in the Basilica.

Fatima Devotions

THE ROSARY

The origins of the Rosary are very old. They go back to the second century of the Christian era.

1. The psalter of Our Fathers, used by hermit monks in the second century as a substitute for the hundred and fifty psalms.

2. In the Eleventh century the monks who couldn't read repeated by heart fifty or a hundred and fifty Our Fathers while their more educated brethren read and meditated on the hundred and fifty psalms. They counted the Our Fathers with pebbles, shells, seeds etc which they moved from one place to another or dropped into a vessel. By the beginning of the twelfth centuy counting beads had aleady appeared.

3. St Dominic of Gusman (1170–1221) founded the Dominican order. He and his companions began to pray the office of Our Lady. While they were doing this he got his illiterate monks to repeat Hail Marys, fifty each time – a third, or *terço*, of the one

132

hundred and fifty which was the full Rosary equal
to a psalter of Hail Marys.

The Rosary is a repetitive prayer, a meaningful verbal
formula.

This type of prayer is not exclusively Catholic,
repetitive prayers are part of all the great non-
Christian religions too – Brahman, Buddhism, Islam,
Judahism. But we must not confuse the Rosary with a
mantra. The Rosary is a prayer complete in itself, not
a means of achieving some lulled mental state. The
word Rosary comes from the Latin, *rosarium*, which
means a garden of roses. The term is used because it is
a devotion in honour of Mary, the Mystical Rose.

In time St Dominic divided the Hail Marys into
groups of ten which he called decades. He arranged
that each decade be introduced by an Our Father and,
at the end, that the Hail Holy Queen should be said.
The separation into decades gave scope to recall and
meditate on episodes in the life of Jesus.

The Joyful Mysteries

(Mondays & Thursdays. Also Sundays from Advent
till Christmas.)
1. The Annunciation.
2. The Visitation.
3. The Nativity.
4. The Presentation.
5. The Finding in the Temple.

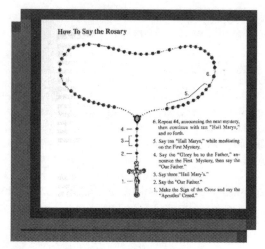

The Sorrowful Mysteries

(Tuesdays & Fridays. Also Sundays of Lent.)
1. The Agony in the Garden.
2. The Scourging at the Pillar.
3. The Crowning with Thorns.
4. The Carrying of the Cross.
5. The Crucifixion.

The Glorious Mysteries

(Wednesdays & Saturdays. Also Sundays from Easter till Advent.)
1. The Resurrection.
2. The Ascension.
3. The Descent of the Holy Ghost.

134

4. The Assumption.
5. The Coronation of Mary.

The Rosary: A Weapon of Peace

Our Lady appeared six times in Fatima in 1917. Each time she asked for the Rosary to be said <u>every day</u>.

13th May: *Pray the Rosary <u>every day</u> in order to obtain peace for the world and the end of the war.*

13th June: *I wish you to pray the Rosary <u>every day</u>.*

13th July: *I want you to continue to pray the Rosary <u>every day</u> in honour of Our Lady of the Rosary in order to obtain peace for the world and the end of the war, because only She can help you.*
   When you pray the Rosary say after each mystery, 'O my Jesus, forgive us our sins, save us from the fire of hell, and lead all souls to heaven especially those who are most in need.'

19th August: *I want you to continue praying the Rosary <u>every day</u>.*

13th September: *Continue to pray the Rosary in order to obtain the end of the war.*

13th October: *I am the Lady of the Rosary. Continue always to pray the Rosary <u>every day</u>.*

The Popes on the Rosary

Leo XIII

The Rosary has this remarkable quality: It has been established mainly to implore the Mother of God for help against the enemies of Christians. No one ignores that it contributed repeatedly to relieve the bad times of the Church. (Lit. Ap. Salutaris ille. 24th Sept. 1883.)

Pius XII

We don't hesitate in repeating: We place our confidence in the Rosary to cure the evils that afflict our times. It is not by force, nor with weapons, nor by human power, but with God's help obtained through this prayer that the Church, strong like David with his sling, may fearlessly face the infernal enemy. (Enc. Ingruentium maiorum, 15th Sept. 1951.)

John XXIII

Blessed be Mary's Rosary. What sweetness we feel upon seeing the rosary beads raised by innocent hands of priests, saints, pure souls, young and elderly people, by all those who appreciate the value and efficacy of prayer, raised by countless crowds as an emblem, and as a sign for peace in the hearts and amidst people. (Apostolic Letter – The Rosary for World Peace, 29th September 1961.)

Paul VI

The Rosary is a way of praying very well adapted to the sense of the people of God, very pleasing to the Mother of God and very powerful to obtain favours from heaven. (Enc. Christi Matri. 15th Sept. 1966.) Without meditation on the mysteries, the Rosary is a body without a soul and its praying is in danger of becoming a mechanical repetition of formulas. (Ex. Marialis Cultus.)

John Paul II

The Rosary is my favourite prayer! Marvellous in its simplicity and in its profundity. In this prayer we repeat very often the words that the Virgin Mary heard from the Angel and Her cousin. All the Church joins in these words. (29th Oct. 1978.)

THE BROWN SCAPULAR

On the night of the 15th–16th July 1251, the English Prior General of the Carmelites, Simon Stock, was praying because it seemed as if the Order might be disbanded. In his prayer he experienced a vision in which he saw angelic choirs and, in their midst, the Blessed Virgin with the scapular of the Order in her hand. She gave it to him with the words, **'This shall be the privilege for you and for all Carmelites, that anyone dying in this habit shall be saved.'**

137

The scapular was the apron of the times – a long strip of cloth, with a hole for the head in the middle, which went over the shoulders to protect from soiling and staining.

As was the custom at the time the Order gave an abbreviated version of their scapular to benefactors and friends until the small, hidden scapular became a symbol of the Carmelite Third Order. Gradually the wearing of what became known as the Brown Scapular grew common among Christians, encouraged by a Papal Bull which was the origin of the idea of the Sabbatine Privilege, that is, that Our Lady would deliver from Purgatory on the Saturday after their death souls who had worn the scapular, followed the Church's fasts, recited the Little Office of the BVM (or the Rosary) and observed chastity according to their state in life.

To wear the scapular is to wear the livery of the Mother of God, to identify with the consecration to Her Immaculate Heart.

The very last of the 'public' apparitions of Fatima was seen only by Lucia. It was Mary as Our Lady of Mount Carmel holding out the Brown Scapular in Her hand. This vision can be interpreted on a number of levels but there is no ignoring the scapular. In 1950 Lucia was asked, 'Why do you think Our Lady appeared with the scapular in the last vision?'

Lucia answered, 'She meant that all Catholics should wear the Scapular as part of the Fatima message. One could not follow this message unless he or she wore the brown Scapular.'

'Is the Scapular as important as the Rosary in fulfill-
ing the Fatima message?'

'Sister Lucia said, 'The Scapular and the Rosary are
inseparable.'

In 1951, in a letter commemorating the seven
hundredth-anniverary of the Scapular, Pius XII
wrote: 'Take this Scapular which Our Lady has given
as a sign of consecration to Her Immaculate Heart. Go
out and convince the world that it must be dedicated
to the Blessed Virgin if it will find peace.'

THE FIVE FIRST SATURDAYS

On 10th December 1925 when Lucia was in her room
on the second storey of the Dorothean convent in
Pontevedra, Spain, the Most Holy Virgin appeared to
her and, by her side, elevated on a luminous cloud,
was a child. The Most Holy Virgin rested Her hand on
Lucia's shoulder and as She did so She showed her a
heart encircled by thorns which She was holding in
Her other hand. At the same time the child said, 'Have
compassion on the Heart of your Most Holy Mother,
covered with thorns, with which ungrateful men
pierce it at every moment, and there is no one to make
an act of reparation to remove them.'

Then the Most Holy Virgin said, 'Look, my
daughter, at my Heart, surrounded with thorns
with which ungrateful men pierce me at every
moment by their blasphemies and ingratitude.
You at least try to console me and say that I

promise to assit at the hour of death, with the graces necessary for salvation, all those who, for five consecutive months, shall confess, receive Holy Communion, recite five decades of the Rosary, and keep me company for fifteen minutes while meditating on the fifteen myster- ies of the Rosary, with the intention of making reparation to me.'

In another encounter when Our Lord appeared to Lucia in the garden of the convent at Pontevedra on 15th February 1926 He said, 'It is true, my daugh- ter, that many souls begin the First Saturdays, but few finish them, and those who do complete them do so in order to receive the graces that are promised thereby. It would please me more if they did Five with fervour and with the intention of making reparation to the Heart of your heav- enly Mother, than if they did Fifteen in a tepid and indifferent manner.'

Conditions

The privilege of the Five First Saturdays is salvation. The following are the conditions:

1. *Confession.* For each first Saturday it is necessary to go to confession with the intention of making repa- ration. This can be done any day before or after the First Saturday as long as Communion is received in grace.

   Lucia asked, what about those who forget to form

this intention of reparation. Jesus replied that they could form it in the next confession, taking advantage of the first opportunity to go to confession.

2. *Communion*, in the state of grace.

3. *The Rosary*.

4. *Meditation* for fifteen minutes on one mystery, various mysteries or all of them. One three minute meditation before each one of the Five mysteries of the Rosary while praying the Rosary.

The devotion of the first Saturdays can, for a justified reason, be made on the following Sunday with the authorisation of a confessor.

In all these practices the intention of consoling the Immaculate Heart of Mary must be taken.

Suggested Prayer for Forming the Intention of Consoling the Immaculate Heart of Mary for the First Saturday Observances

Holy Virgin, my dear Mother, I hear with sorrow the complaints of Your Heart surrounded by thorns, which ungrateful men are always piercing with blasphemy and ingratitude.

Touched by the burning desire to love You as my Mother and to promote a tender devotion to Your Immaculate Heart, I prostrate myself at Your feet to show you the pity I feel for the pain which many souls have caused. I humbly offer You my prayers and sacrifices to repair the sins by which ungrateful men respond to Your love. For them and for me obtain from Jesus forgiveness of all these sins, for but one word from You can give us all the grace of conversion. Hasten, O Virgin Mother, the conversion of poor sinners so that they may love Jesus truly and leave off offending Our Lord, who has already been very much offended, and so avoid damnation.

Cast upon me Your look of mercy so that I may love God with all my heart, here on earth, and forever in heaven. Amen.

THE CONSECRATION OF RUSSIA TO THE IMMACULATE HEART OF MARY

Shortly after the Pontevedra Apparitions in which Our Lady asked for the First Five Saturday Communions, Lucia was moved to Tuy, on the Spanish side of the Minho River. She made her first profession of religious vows on 3rd October 1928. On 13th June the following year she received a second communication from Our Lady, promised in July 1917 when She said, '**I shall come to ask for the consecration of Russia to my Immaculate Heart.**'

Here is Lucia's own account: 'I had asked for and

obtained permission from my superiors to make a Holy Hour from 11 p.m. to midnight during the night of Thursday–Friday. Being alone I knelt in the middle of the balustrade which is in the centre of the chapel to recite, prostrate, the prayers of the angel. Feeling tired, I got up and continued to recite them with arms outstretched. The only light was that of the sanctuary lamp. Suddenly the whole chapel lit up as by a supernatural light, and there appeared on the altar a cross of light which rose up as far as the ceiling. In this very clear light one could see on the upper part of the cross the figure of a man from the waist upwards and on his chest was the figure of a dove, also luminous. Nailed to the cross was another man. A little below his waist, suspended in the air, one could see a chalice and a large host upon which there fell several drops of blood which flowed from the cheeks of the crucified one, and from a wound in his chest. Flowing over the host, these drops fell into the chalice.

'Under the right arm of the cross was Our Lady (it was Our Lady of Fatima with Her Immaculate Heart in Her left hand without sword or roses, but with a crown of thorns and flames). Under the left arm of the cross, large letters of crystalline water flowed down over the altar and formed these words GRACE AND MERCY. I understood that the mystery of the Most Holy Trinity had been shown to me and I received enlightenment upon this mystery which it is not permitted to me to reveal.

'Our Lady then said me, "**The moment has come in which God asks the Holy Father, in union with**

all the Bishops of the world, to make the consecration of Russia to My Immaculate Heart,
promising to save it by this means. There are so
many souls whom the justice of God condemns
for sins committed against Me, that I have come
to ask for reparation: sacrifice yourself for this
intention and pray."

'Later, through an intimate communication in
August 1931, Our Lord complained: "They have not
chosen to heed My request ... Like the King of
France, they will regret it and then will do it, but
it will be too late. Russia will already have
spread her errors throughout the world, provok-
ing wars and persecutions against the Church.
The Holy Father will have much to suffer."'

Commentators interpret the reference to the
request to the King of France to refer to the failure of
Louis XIV to consecrate France to The Sacred Heart
as revealed by St Margaret Mary Alacoque. The
French Revolution was the outcome.

Lucia made her final vows as a Dorothean in Tuy on
3rd October 1934. Her mother travelled there for the
occasion but it was the last time they were to meet.
Her mother died in Aljustrel on 16th July 1942, the
feast of Our Lady of Carmel, who had appeared to
Lucia in the sky during the Miracle of the Sun.

On 25th January 1938 the *night illumined by an
unknown light* (which Our Lady had foretold during
the July 1917 Apparition, just after she had given the

children a glimpse of hell but told them at the time to keep it secret) was seen all over Europe and recorded in all the observatories. Contemporary descriptions speak of this atmospheric phenomenon as *a blood-red glow* and *a red rainbow*. Emphasis was also put on the terrible impression that this aurora had made on individuals. In France it was particularly noticeable in the Alps and in Brittany where people concluded that a Second World War was at hand.

On 31st October 1942 Pope Pius XII consecrated the world to the Immaculate Heart of Mary in a Portuguese language radio broadcast. He didn't specifically mention Russia, which might have been politically imprudent at the time, but referred to 'those peoples separated by error and discord'. Lucia later commented, however, that the consecration was not in accord with what Our Lady had asked for in as much as it lacked the participation of the Bishops representing the entire body of the Faithful.

On 13th May 1946 the Papal Legate, Cardinal Masella, crowned Our Lady of Fatima Queen of the World on behalf of Pope Pius XII.

On 25th May 1946 Lucia was posted to the College of the Sacred Heart of Jesus of Sardão in Vila Nova de Gaia, across the river from Porto.

Having obtained permission from Pius XII to embrace the contemplative life she entered the Carmelite

Convent in Coimbra on 25th March 1948. As a Carmelite she is known as Sister Maria of the Immaculate Heart.

One attempt by Pope John XXIII in 1960 to make the consecration to the Immaculate Heart in the sanctuary at Fatima failed because the Pope himself wasn't present.

In 1965 Pope Paul VI made an unexpected consecration at the last assembly of the Vatican II Council. Although the bishops were present its very spontaneity made it invalid because of the lack of consensus with the people of God.

On 13th May 1982 Pope John Paul II made a consecration in Fatima when offering his would-be assassin's bullet to the shrine but as this, too, was without the participation of the bishops, Sister Lucia said that it was invalid.

On the feast of the Annunciation, 25th March 1984, in Rome, kneeling before the same statue of Our Lady of Fatima which is venerated in the Chapel of the Apparitions, Pope John Paul II renewed the Consecration of the World to the Immaculate Heart of Mary, with substantially the same formula he used in Fatima on 13th May 1982. This same act was realised by bishops in all the dioceses of the world.

The then Bishop of Leiria-Fatima, Alberto Cosme do Amaral, who was in Rome for the Ceremony later said, 'During the actual Consecration there were a few moments of pause during which it was not clear what the Holy Father said. Later I thanked the Pope for consecrating the world to the Immaculate Heart of Mary and the Pope added, "and Russia!"' Bishop Amaral continued with a telling sentence, 'A moral totality of the world's bishops joined the Pope in this collegial consecration, including Eastern Orthodox bishops.'

In 1992 The writer on Fatima, Carlos Evaristo, asked Sister Lucia in the Coimbra Carmel, 'But did not Russia have to be specifically mentioned, and did not Our Lady say this?' And the seer answered, 'The Pope's intention was Russia, when he said, "those peoples ..." in the text of the 1984 consecration. Those who knew of the request for the consecration of Russia, knew what he was referring to as did God, who is all knowledgeable and can read the minds of men. God knew that the Pope's intention was Russia and that he meant Russia in the consecration. What is important is the intention, like when a priest has the intention to consecrate a Host. Our Lady never requested that Russia be specifically mentioned by name. At the time I didn't even know what Russia was. We thought she was a very wicked woman. What matters is the Pope's intention and the Bishops knew that the intention the Pope had was to consecate Russia.'

Also, after the Consecration, Sister Lucia was visited by the Apostolic Nuncio and, in an interview with her published in the *Fatima Family Messenger*,

October 1989, she reported that he asked her, 'Is Russia now consecrated?'

'Yes, now it is.'

'Now we wait for the miracle?'

'God will keep his word.'

Also in 1989 Sister Lucia wrote a private letter, which she later gave permission to be printed in the *International Catholic Journal* 30 Days (issue of March 1990) in which she explained that previous consecrations had not been effective because they had not been carried out in union with all the bishops. The letter continues, 'It was later made by the present Pontiff, John Paul II, on 25th March 1984, after he wrote to all the bishops of the world, asking that each of them make the consecration in his own diocese with the people of God who had been entrusted to him. The Pope asked that the statue of Our Lady of Fatima be brought to Rome and he did it publicly in union with all the bishops who, with His Holiness, were uniting themselves with the people of God, the Mystical Body of Christ; and it was made to the Immaculate Heart of Mary, Mother of Christ and of His Mystical Body, so that, with Her and through Her with Christ, the consecration could be carried and offered to the Father for the salvation of humanity. Thus the consecration was made by His Holiness Pope John Paul II on 25th March 1984.'

(In other private correspondence Sister Lucia further revealed that the 1984 consecration had prevented a nuclear war that would otherwise have taken place in 1985.) The sudden evaporation of

Soviet Communism towards the end of the twentieth century is too well known to need repeating here.

THE CONSECRATION OF THE MILLENNIUM TO OUR LADY

On Friday 6th October 2000 the statue of Our Lady of Fatima was taken from Fatima to Rome accompanied by the Bishop of Leiria-Fatima, Serafim da Silva. It was taken immediately from Ciampino airport to the Chapel in the Papal appartments in the Vatican.

On 7th October, a First Saturday and the Feast Day of Our Lady of the Rosary, the statue was taken to St Peter's Basilica at 9 a.m. for the veneration of the faithful. In the evening it was taken into the Square in Procession. At 8 p.m. the Holy Father, in union with all the bishops, prayed the Rosary. During this time there was a satellite link up with the shrine of Our Lady of Guadalupe in Mexico, and Fatima in Portugal. The leading of the five mysteries of the Rosary was entrusted successively to representatives – a Cardinal, a Bishop, a family – of the five Continents, in this order: Oceania, Asia, America, Africa, Europe.

The fifth decade was led by Sr. Lucy and the sisters from the Carmelite Monastery of Coimbra, Portugal, connected with St Peter's Square. (This had been recorded in Coimbra some months earlier.) After the recitation of the Rosary, the Holy Father addressed the bishops assembled for the Jubilee and members of the faithful while a floral tribute to Our Lady of

Fatima was presented by three Portuguese shepherd children and the choir sang the *Salve Regina*. Later the Statue was taken to the Sisters of the cloistered monastery 'Ecclesia Mater' in the Vatican.

On Sunday 8th October, following the Mass in St Peter's Square, The Holy Father – in front of the statue of Our Lady of Fatima – consecrated, in union with the Bishops, the Church, the World and the New Millennium to Our Blessed Lady. After spending the day in St Peter's Square the statue was returned to the Papal Chapel.

On Monday morning Cardinal Secretary of State, Angelo Sodano, presided at a farewell ceremony in the San Damaso courtyard, after which the statue was taken to Fiumicino airport for the return to Portugal.

The Text of the Act of Entrustment of the Third Millennium to Mary Most Holy

by Pope John Paul II at the Jubilee of the Bishops, Rome, 8th October 2000

'Woman, behold your son!' (John 19:26). As we near the end of this Jubilee Year, when you, O Mother, have offered us Jesus anew, the blessed fruit of your womb most pure, the Word made flesh, the world's Redeemer, we hear more clearly the sweet echo of his words entrusting us to you, making you our Mother: 'Woman, behold your son!'

When he entrusted to you the Apostle John, and

with him the children of the Church and all people, Christ did not diminish but affirmed anew the role which is his alone as the Saviour of the world. You are the splendour which in no way dims the light of Christ, for you exist in him and through him. Everything in you is fiat: you are the Immaculate One, through you there shines the fullness of grace. Here, then, are your children gathered before you at the dawn of the new millennium. The church today, through the voice of the Successor of Peter, in union with so many Pastors assembled here from every corner of the world, seeks refuge in your motherly protection and trustingly begs your intercession as she faces the challenges which lie hidden in the future.

In this year of grace, countless people have known the overflowing joy of the mercy which the Father has given us in Christ. In the particular churches throughout the world, and still more in this centre of Christianity, the widest array of people have accepted this gift. Here the enthusiasm of the young rang out, here the sick have lifted up their prayer. Here have gathered priests and religious, artists and journalists, workers and people of learning, children and adults, and all have acknowledged in your beloved Son the Word of God made flesh in your womb. O Mother, intercede for us, that the fruits of this Year will not be lost and that the seeds of grace will grow to the full measure of the holiness to which we are all called.

Today we wish to entrust to you the future that awaits us, and we ask you to be with us on our way. We are the men and women of an extraordinary time, exhilarating yet full of contradictions. Humanity now has instruments of unprecedented power: we can turn this world into a garden, or reduce it to a pile of rubble. We have devised the astounding capacity to intervene in the very well-springs of life: man can use this power for good, within the bounds of the moral law, or he can succumb to the short-sighted pride of a science which accepts no limits, but tramples on the respect due to every human being. Today as never before in the past, humanity stands at a crossroads. And once again, O Virgin Most Holy, salvation lies fully and uniquely in Jesus, your Son.

Therefore, O Mother, like the Apostle John, we wish to take you into our home (cf. John 19:27), that we may learn from you to become like your Son. 'Woman, behold your son!' Here we stand before you to entrust to your maternal care ourselves, the Church, the entire world. Plead for us with your beloved Son that he may give us in abundance the Holy Spirit, the Spirit of Truth which is the fountain of life. Receive the Spirit for us and with us, as happened in the first community gathered round you in Jerusalem on the day of Pentecost (cf. Acts 1:14). May the Spirit open our hearts to justice and love, and guide people and nations to mutual understanding and a firm desire for peace. We entrust to you all people, beginning with the weakest: the babies yet unborn, and those born into poverty and suffering, the young in search of meaning, the unemployed, and those suffering hunger and disease. We entrust to you all

152

troubled families, the elderly with no one to help them, and all who are alone and without hope.

O Mother, you know the sufferings and hopes of the Church and the world: come to the aid of your children in the daily trials which life brings to each one, and grant that, thanks to the efforts of all, the darkness will not prevail over the light. To you, Dawn of Salvation, we commit our journey through the new Millennium, so that with you as guide all people may know Christ, the light of the world and its only Saviour, who reigns with the Father and the Holy Spirit for ever and ever. Amen.

Convents and Religious Associations

Monastic walls are thick and stout,
They're there to keep the worldly out;
If the wordly knew what joys they hide
They'd break them down to get inside.

In Fatima there are something like sixty-five convents of female religious and fifteen of male. Fifteen of the convents of religious sisters are equipped to accommodate pilgrims. Of the houses of male religious eight offer accommodation.

All houses have their own chapels; many have regular Masses and exposition of the Blessed Sacrament. However, to list the convents and times of services might make them seem like public facilities. Unless the individual pilgrim is actually staying in one of the houses, or has some personal contact with a particular congregation, there are sufficient openings for all liturgical, non-liturgical and private devotions in the *Santuário*.

The International, English-speaking foundation, the Monastery of Pius XII, Rua do Rosario 1, Lomba d'Équa, is the one religious house in Fatima where readers of this guide will have no communication problems. The community, Dominican Nuns of the

Perpetual Rosary, have been here since 1954. At that time three American sisters came to do the pioneering work and were soon joined by four more Americans, two Irish and one English sister. Currently there are Irish, English, American, Singapore, Italian and Australian nuns living the full monastic life in the convent. There is Mass in the church at 08.00 each morning (09.00 on Sundays) and Exposition of the Blessed Sacrament all day until the church closes after Benediction which starts after Vespers, around 17.50. The Portuguese language is used for most Masses (English on Friday) and for the chanting of the Divine Office.

The nuns are enclosed but one can visit them and speak through the grille and they have the only outlet for a range of English language books on the Fatima phenonmenon. Portuguese ladies look after the door. Ring the bell and tell them you'd like to look at the books. Around 10.00 in the morning, or 16.00 in the afternoon are usually convenient times.

Religious Houses Providing Accommodation for Pilgrims

Convents of Female Religious:
Congr. Nª Sª Caridade do Bom Pastor
(Congregation of Our Lady of Charity of the Good Shepherd)
Rua do Coração de Maria, 27
249 53 13 29

Institute Secular das Cooperadoras da Família
Rua Mons. Joaquim Alves Brás
249 53 23 89

Franciscanas Miss. Mãe Divino Pastor
(Franciscan Missionaries of the Mother of the Divine
Shepherd)
Rua do Coração do Maria, 25
249 53 12 83

Irmãs Concepcionistas
Rua do Anjo de Portugal, 8
249 53 12 78

Filhas da Caridade de S. Vincente de Paulo
(Daughters of Charity of St Vincent de Paul)
Rua S. Vincente de Paulo, 25
249 53 12 19

Irmas Dominicanas Portugesas
(Congregation of the Dominican Sisters of St
Catherine of Sienna)
Rua Francisco Marto, 50
249 53 33 17

Congregação das Filhas da Igreja
(Congregation of the Daughters of the Church)
Rua do Anjo de Portugal, 20
249 53 14 15

Congregação das Servas Franciscanas de Nª Sª das
Graças
(Franciscan Sisters of Our Lady of Graces)
Rua Anjo de Portugal, 25
249 53 23 95

Eucharistic Missionaries of Nazaré
Rua Anjo de Portugal, 7
249 53 12 27

Religiosas Reparadores de Nª Sª das Dores de Fátima
(Reparation Sisters of Our Lady of Sorrows)
Rus Francisco Marto, 203
249 53 10 90

Congregação das Servas de Maria Reparadores
(The Servants of Mary Reparation Sisters)
Rua do Coração de Maria, 24
249 53 13 95

Companhia de Stª Teresa de Jesus
(Teresian Sisters)
Rua do Rasário
249 53 14 82

Reparation Missionaries of the Sacred Heart of Jesus
Centro Catequético – Ave. Beato Nuno Nº129
249 53 12 76

Houses of Male Religious:
Ordem Hospitaleira de S. João de Jesus
Brothers of St John of God
Rua de S. João de Deus
249 53 17 57

Ordem dos Frades Menores Capuchinhos
(Capuchin Fathers)
Ave. Beato Nuno, 405
249 53 12 87

Carmelite Fathers
Casa Beato Nuno
Ave. Beato Nuno, 271
Apartado 4
249 53 30 69   (Fax) 249 53 27 57

Congregação do Verbo Divino
(Divine Word Fathers)
Seminário do Verbo Divino
Rotunda Norte
Apartado 2
249 53 2163/249 53 21 73

Marianos Fathers
Rua de S. Paulo, 2
249 53 13 89

Consolata Missionary Fathers
Seminário da Consolata
Rua Francisco Marto
Apartardo 5
249 53 21 18/249 53 29 81

Padres Mis. Do Coração de Maria
(Missionary Fathers of the Heart of Mary)
(Claretians)
Ave. Beato Nuno, 291
Moita Redonda
249 53 11 69

Silenciosos Operáios da Cruz
Silent Operations of the Cross
Estrada de Torres Novas
249 52 17 77

THE *SERVITAS* AND THE MESSENGER OF FATIMA MOVEMENT

The <u>Servita</u> is humble, is patient, doesn't seek his own satisfaction, loves to be silent, hidden, ignored; he embraces the cross in its entirety, without relief, without attracting attention, without consolation. He knows and seeks only one joy, the joy of serving like Jesus, like Mary.

The Episcopal Decree of Approval
Leiria 13th September 1983

Two organisations exist to assist in the caring for Pilgrims to the Shrine and to promote the Fatima message in their own lives. The work in the Shrine and in Portuguese parishes necessarily restricts membership to people living in Portugal. These are the *Servitas* and the Message of Fatima Movement.

The *Servitas* was created in 1924 by the Bishop of Leiria to be an association with canonical rights, composed of the laity, religious and priests. They pledge to strive for the sanctification of the world, starting with themselves, like a yeast working from the inside, showing Christ to others by the testament of their own life, radiating their faith, their hope and their charity.

The *Servitas* promise to spread the message of Our Lady and of the Angel of Portugal. They willingly collaborate with the Santuário in serving the pilgrims, ensuring that they are made to feel as brothers and fostering the spirit which gave life to their pilgrimage. Currently they work in the sanctuary during the great pilgrimages and on all other occasions when their assistance is called for. They organise and direct the pilgrims, keeping peace and order. They assit in the Capelinha, at the pyre, in the Capela de Reconciliação. They work at the First Aid centre and help the sick when they are admitted into the Casa dos Dores and when they receive the Sacrament and the Blessing.

When they are on duty the *Servitas* can be recognised by their insignias. The ladies are in a white suit with a blue star on the veil, the cross of Christ at the breast and a blue armband. The men wear shoulder-belts. The medics have white smocks and yellow armbands bearing the words *Medica Servita*. The priests' white armbands read *Sacerdote Servita*. The religious have their habits and armbands. *Servitas* candidates wear blue or red armbands which display the words *Servita Auxiliar*.

The *Message of Fatima Movement* is an organisation of formulation and apostolate, instituted by the Portuguese Episcopal Conference which approved its constitution in July 1984. Its object is to promote the message of Fatima. It succeeds the Pious Union of the Crusaders of Our Lady of Fatima and assumes the rights and obligations of that organisation. The movement fulfils its mission in three fields – the apostolate of Prayer, the apostolate of pilgrimage and the apostolate of mission. It is active in 60% of Portuguese parishes and has around 200,000 associates of whom 117,000 receive the journal *Voz de Fátima*. Any practising Catholic can belong to this movement.

The Movement's headquarters is in the Santuário, behind the Capelinha.

Gifts to the Sanctuary

Over the years many gifts have been given to the Sanctuary, to pay homage to Our Lady, or to beg Her intercession, or to thank Her for favours received. The moveable objects are kept in a safe in the Basilica though a facility which would make them available to be seen by pilgrims is planned. Mention has been made elsewhere in this book of some of them.

The English Chalice
The Austrian Lausperene
The Hungarian Santa Cruz and Calvary
The German Statue of Pius XII
The Singapore Arch Mosaic
The Pectoral Cross of Cardinal Roncalli
The Portuguese Crown
The American Statue of the Immaculate Heart
The Golden Rose
The Ring of Pope John-Paul II
The Irish Monstrance

Below we give details of the last five of the gifts listed here:

The Crown

A Gift from the Women of Portugal

The principal crown for the statue of Our Lady of Fatima is currently kept in the treasury which is above the sacristy in the Basilica. It was a gift from the women of Portugal in thanksgiving for their country's preservation from the Spanish Civil War and the Second World War and was presented on 13th October 1942. It is gold, weighs 1.2 kilos, is encrusted with 313 pearls and 2,679 precious stones, rubies, emeralds, turquoises etc. Made by *Leitão Brothers* of Lisbon, it took twelve jewellery artists, working unpaid, two to three months to complete.

It is only placed on the statue's head on the major pilgrimage days, 13th of each month from May to October. It is taken from the treasury to the Capelinha before the 09.15 Rosary and put on the statue which is taken in procession to the Recinto altar at 10.00. The statue with the crown remains on its float of flowers on the south side of the altar throughout the Mass and the Benediction of the Sick. After the ceremonies at the Recinto altar comes the Procissão do Adeus to the Capelinha where the crown is exchanged for the one used for daily wear around two o'clock and returned to the treasury.

On 13th May 1982 Pope John Paul II celebrated Mass at the Recinto altar in Fatima. In the course of his homily he said:

And so I come here today because on this very day last year, in St Peter's Square in Rome, the attempt on the Pope's life was made, in mysterious coincidence with the anniversary of the first apparitition of Fatima, which occurred on 13th May 1917.

I seemed to recognise in the coincidence of the dates a special call to come to this place which the Mother of God seems to have chosen in a particular way.

The Holy Father then presented to the Shrine the actual bullet which had been fired at him and had been inexplicably diverted from his chest and fell to the floor of the vehicle he was in. This was later secured into the crown under the central orb where it still remains, a moving testimony to Papal solidarity with the Portuguese in their faith in the Fatima apparitions.

The Statue of the Immaculate Heart in the Niche in the Front of the Basilica

A Gift from the Catholic People of The United States of America

In 1947 when the American priest/sculptor, Thomas McGlynn OP showed the three-foot cast statue of The Immaculate Heart of Mary he had made under the supervision of Sister Lucia to the Bishop of Leiria, he had just seen the half-built Basilica in Cova da Iria. He wanted to ask the Bishop if he could make a much larger one for the niche. The Bishop, however, made no particular comment on the statue in front of him and Fr. McGlynn was too discouraged to ask. At the last minute an Irish Dominican who was with him, Fr. Gardiner, conscious that Sister Lucia was praying for just that intention, put the question to the Bishop. The Bishop answered that he could make one for a niche inside the Basilica but that the outside niche was already spoken for.

The following day he was taking some pictures of the shrine when a boy interrupted to say that the Bishop had come up from Leiria and wanted to see the American priest. Fr. McGlynn went to meet him. The Bishop simply said that he had decided to ask him, Fr. McGlynn, to make the statue. He gave no explanation for his sudden change of decision.

When word got about in America that Fr. McGlynn was to make the statue, gifts of money for the work it would involve came in from all over the United States. The graceful statue, so simple in its lines and with an attitude of such tenderness and maternal care, is a great tribute to the way many American Catholics have taken and continue to take the message of Fatima to their hearts.

Father McGlynn worked on the statue at Pietrasanta, near Pisa, in Italy from 7.3.56–5.4.58.
The statue was blessed by D. João Pereira Venâncio on 13.5.58.

The Golden Rose

22nd January 1965. It was announced at the official Mass that the Holy Father had granted the Golden Rose to the Sanctuary of Fatima.

12th May 1965. The Golden Rose was presented to the Sanctuary of Fatima by Cardinal Cento on behalf of the Pope, Paul VI. Twenty-five Portuguese bishops were present as well as the Cardinal Patriarch of Lisbon.

The Golden Rose is a Papal gift. Originally it was a single flower of wrought gold, tinted red. Over the centuries it has gone through many variations till at the present day it is a branch with several flowers and leaves, and with the principal flower on top, all of pure gold. Innocent III gave it scriptural dignity when, adverting to its spiritual resemblance in a sermon, he said that the rose is the flower spoken of by Isaiah (XI.i): *There shall come forth a rod out of the root of Jesse, and a flower shall rise up out of his root.*

It is blessed on Laetare Sunday – the fourth Sunday in Lent – but it is not always a new one that is blessed; the old one is used until it is given away, and that can be presented to any person, place, institution, city or state that the Pontiff wishes to honour. The practice seems to have arisen around the thirteenth century.

Napoleon III, Queen Marie Amélie of Portugal, the Republic of Lucca, the Laterna Basilica, the Sanctuary of Loreto and St Marks in Venice have all been recipients. King Henry VIII of England received three and one was also received by his daughter Mary Tudor.

The Ring of Pope John Paul II

On the evening of 12th May 2000 when the Holy Father arrived in Fatima – he was to beatify Francisco and Jacinta the following day – he went directly from the football pitch, which had been converted into a helicopter pad, to the Capelinha. Here he knelt in prayer before the statue of Our Lady of Fatima which marks the site where Our Heavenly Mother appeared to the young shepherds eighty-three years earlier.

The million pilgrims who packed the Sanctuary, or watched on the giant screens erected behind the Jubilee Wall, saw the Holy Father stand and reach out to an area at the base of the statue. Those who were close enough could see that he was placing a small red box at the feet of the Virgin, and that he left it there.

Later it was revealed that the box contained a ring which had been given to him by the great Polish cardinal, Stefan Wyszynski (1901–1981) on his election to the Chair of Peter in 1978. Cardinal Wyszynski had told the new Pope at the time, 'If God has chosen you, it is to bring the Church into the next millennium.'

With the ring was a written message which translated, reads, *This ring, with the effigy of Our Lady and the words 'Totus Tuus' was given to me by Cardinal Stefan Wyszynski, during the first days of my pontificate. With much joy I offer it to Our Lady of Fatima as a sign*

167

of my profound gratitude for the protection which She has afforded me.

The gift of the ring to Our Lady of Fatima doubtless has significance for our Polish Pope on many different levels, most of which only time will elucidate for us.

The Irish Monstrance

A Gift from the People of Ireland

What is widely regarded as among the most magnificent works of religious art produced in Ireland since the Book of Kells is also one of the most valued religious objects in the Treasury of the Sanctuary of Our Lady of Fatima.

It was the idea of the late Mrs Kathleen Conroy of County Mayo. In the 1940s Kathleen had received a special favour through the intercession of Our Lady and she was anxious to show her gratitude in a tangible way. Remembering that her family, who were from Kilmurry, near Crossmolina in County Mayo, had once presented a monstrance to their local church, she conceived the idea of presenting the developing shrine of Our Lady of Fatima in Portugal with a Monstrance. It was to be especially designed to incorporate aspects of the apparitions, and of Ireland, as the donor nation.

Kathleen and her husband, Keiran, entrusted the manufacture of the Monstrance to the Dublin firm of Gunnings but the original design had to be repeatedly altered because, although there was no public appeal for support, word got round and precious jewellery, gold and cash began to pour in from all over Ireland. The craftsmen at Gunnings worked ceaselessly on the project for almost a year and finally, in 1949, this indescribably beautiful work of religious art emerged from their workshops. It was first put on public display in Dublin and attracted thousands of admirers.

On 7th October 1949, the feast of Our Lady of the Rosary, the Monstrance was formally presented to the Sanctuary of Fatima by a well known Fatima devotee, Dr Finbar Ryan, OP, who at the time was Bishop of Port of Spain in Trinidad. For the occasion four hundred and fifty Irish pilgrims travelled to Fatima by boat and train. At the time it was the largest group of foreign pilgrims to visit the shrine from any country outside the Iberian peninsula.

A Description of the Monstrance

The Monstrance is 42 inches high and weighs 17 pounds. It is made of solid silver, richly covered in gold, and contains about 1700 precious jewels. Around the rim of the base a Latin inscription is chased into the gold:

ddd in festo Ssmi Rosarii ad MDCCCCXLIX Carissimae Matri Filios apud Fatimam immaculato ex corde adlocutae Hiberni pii quo benedictum fructum ventris nobis ostendat.

The devoted Irish dedicated this gift on the Feast of the Most Holy Rosary AD 1949 to a dearly beloved Mother, who has spoken to her children at Fatima from her

Immaculate Heart, that by it (the monstrance) she may show unto us the blessed fruit of her womb.

The base itself consists of four panels representing the four provinces of Ireland. Each panel is heavily gilded with Celtic ornamentation, and each has a separate figure.

The front panel is a beautifully jewelled figure of St Patrick.

The rear panel depicts St Brigid. St Brigid establishes a special link with Portugal because it is widely believed that her mother was Portuguese.[4]

The two side panels each depict a dove, representing two of the three miraculous doves of Our Lady of Fatima, based on an event which had occurred in December 1946 when Portugal was celebrating the three-hundredth anniversary of the dedication of the Country to the Immaculate Conception.[5] (The third dove is incorporated in the Holy Spirit symbol at the top of the Monstrance.)

---

[4] Since the twelfth century St Brigid's head has been preserved at Lumiar, a Lisbon suburb west of the airport, in the Church of São João Baptista.

[5] The statue of Our Lady of Fatima left the Cova da Iria for Lisbon in 1946. 'On this occasion, white doves let loose by someone in the crowd, fluttered down to rest at the feet of the statue and remained there for days without food or drink, oblivious to the jostling crowds, blaring bands and the long road and river journey back to Fatima.' The *Miracle of the Doves* as everyone called it, was later repeated in Brazil during an imposing ceremony in honour of Our Lady of Fatima. From *Fatima – The Great Sign* by Francis Johnston. See 'The Doves of Bombarral' p. 174.

The bottom step of the base is set with a dozen large amethysts. Rising from this part of the base, stretching out between the four panels, are branches representing the stems of the holm-oak tree on which Our Lady stood. The stems burst out at the top of the base to form the foliage, on which rested the feet of Our Lady.

The shaft of the Monstrance, which rises from the foliage, forms the figure of Our Lady, carved with the precise detail of Her Miraculous (the term was used by Pius XII) statue which stands in the Chapel of the Apparitions at the exact spot where She appeared in 1917. Her cloak in the Monstrance figure is studded with diamonds, while Her crown is set with sapphires.

Immediately above Our Lady's crown is a solid gold cross. This is the cross of the fifteen decade Rosary which encircles the Monstrance. Each Our Father bead is a bright red ruby while each of the one hundred and fifty Hail Mary beads is a beautiful diamond.

The plaque or medal of the Rosary depicts the Sacred Heart. This plaque is guarded on each side by embossed representations of the Immaculate Heart of Mary, pierced by a sword, on the right, and the Sacred Heart of Jesus, crushed with thorns, on the left.

The rays of the Monstrance number one hundred and sixty-five the number of beads in a fifteen decade rosary, and inset into the rays are eight panels bearing chased representations of eight of the invocations of the Litany of Loreto, using some Irish historical Christian symbols. Starting from the bottom right and moving clockwise, we find:

1. Singular Vessel of Devotion
2. Gate of heaven
3. House of Gold
4. Mystical Rose
5. Morning Star
6. Tower of Ivory
7. Seat of Wisdom
8. Ark of the Covenant

Numbers 1, 4, 5 and 8 are studded with diamonds and rubies.

The centre wealth of the Monstrance is in the form of a Celtic cross with a silver plaque at each corner, representing the apparitions in Fatima on 13th October 1917.

At the top is a plaque of Our Lady appearing to the three visionaries.

On the left side is the Virgin Mary robed as Our Lady of Mount Carmel.

On the right is the Holy Family group.

The bottom plaque represents Our Lady of Sorrows.

The rims of the Celtic cross are set with some of the generously jewelled gold rings that were donated, still in their original form. So, too, are the outside and inside circles surrounding the Host. Forming a nimbus around the Host are twelve jewelled stars and these are bound together with chased Celtic panels. Surmounting the whole Monstrance is the dove. This has a three-fold significance. Primarily, of course, it represents the Holy Spirit with the Seven Gifts radiating downwards into the Monstrance. The bird, as we have seen, also represents the third of the three miraculous doves associated with Fatima. Finally, the seven red rubies at the tips of the rays are intended to convey seven drops of blood, that is, the Seven Sorrows of Our Lady, reminding us that She appeared at Fatima as Our Lady of Sorrows.

The lunette which holds the Sacred Host is made from solid 18ct gold.

A *custos* – a standing lunette box – which matches the design of the Monstrance, was part of the original presentation to the Shrine. The base of the custos is also four-panelled. The panels are chased with Celtic work and show:

St Patrick's Bell
St Brigid's Cross
The Ardagh Chalice
The Shamrock

The Doves of Bombarral

From 1646 until Manuel II was deposed in 1910 no Portuguese monarch has ever worn a crown. And the reason is this. In 1646 King João IV, before the entire court at Vila Viçosa, took the crown from his own head and placed it at the feet of a statue of the Blessed Virgin and declared that she was to be the Queen and Patroness of Portugal under the title of the Immaculate Conception. Then, by oath, he bound himself and his successors to defend the dogma that the Blessed Virgin was conceived free from original sin. The event was inscribed on stone tablets in every town in the land and Portugal became *A Terra de Nossa Senhora*.

1946 marked the third centenary of the reign of Our Blessed Lady over the country and there were festivities up and down the land. There were two high points to these celebrations. The first was on 13th May when it is estimated that up to, and perhaps over, a million pilgrims gathered at Cova da Iria to witness the personal Legate of Pope Pius XII, Cardinal Aloisio Benedetto Masella, place a precious crown on the head of the little statue of Our Lady of Fatima. The gold and the precious stones that went into the making of the crown, as we have seen, were freely given by the women of Portugal from their personal jewel caskets. The kings no longer sat on the thrones but the Immaculate Conception, the Queen of Portugal, still reigned, under the additional title of Our Lady of Fatima.

The second high point was on 8th December 1946, the feast of the Immaculate Conception. It was decided that the statue would be taken from Fatima to Lisbon in solemn procession. In Lisbon, in the ancient cathedral, the *Sé*, in the name of the hierarchy, the Government of the Republic and the People of Portugal, the Cardinal Patriarch of Lisbon would formally renew the consecration of the nation to the Immaculate Conception.

The procession started out from Fatima on 22nd November. The platform that bore the statue was two metres long and one metre wide. On it steps were built up to a height of 1.3 metres where the statue was secured. The whole platform was covered with white flowers and it was carried for the whole fifteen days of its ninety mile journey on the shoulders of willing men. All along the route there were demonstrations of homage, affection and loyalty. Each town staged formal receptions, both civil and religious. The statue spent the nights in churches where it was venerated in all-night vigils. Each morning, after Mass, its journey was resumed.

Today a fine motorway links Fatima with Lisbon and a car journey takes little over an hour. But in 1946 the road was a tortuous one, zigzagging down to Batalha, south west to the magnificent old Cisterican

Monastery of Alcobaca, further south to Caldas da Raínha – the Queens's thermal spa – on to Obidos and then to Bombarral which is on a level with the city of Santarem, but near the Atlantic coast.

A lady who lived in Bombarral, Dona Maria Emilia Martins Campos, had planned a special personal welcome which involved a triumphal arch across the street, bedecked with flowers and surmounted by a crown. Inside the crown were to be six white doves and at the moment of the statue's passing beneath the arch the doves would be released by means of a connecting cord. It would be a charming tribute to the Queen of Portugal. Dona Maria wrote to a friend in Lisbon asking her to buy six white doves. The friend bought the doves for seventy-eight escudos in the Praça da Figuera in Central Lisbon and sent them on 29th November.

The procession was to reach Bombarral on 1st December. Because of time and various circumstances the arch could not be built. Furthermore one of the doves had died in transit. Ever resourceful Dona Maria dressed two little girls fittingly and had them go out before the statue and set the five doves free. One of them flew away. The other four flew to the statue and settled in the flowers at its feet. The statue bearers tried to shoo the birds away, fearing they might soil the statue and disarrange the flowers. When they were flushed out they simply circled the statue and returned. Eventually their persistence won out and they were permitted to remain without interference though one flew off near Torres Vedras and did not return. The remaining three stayed on the steps at the foot of the statue for the five days it took to travel from Bombarral to Lisbon. Occasionally one would fly off to find food but very soon it would be back nestling among the flowers. Nothing disturbed them, not the noise of the jubilant crowds, the fire-crackers (a mandatory feature of any Portuguese festivity), the rain, the wind, the December cold or the aeroplanes that swooped down from the sky on the outskirts of Lisbon to shower the statue with petals.

Initially the statue was taken to the then new church of Our Lady of Fatima which can be found off the Avenida de Berna between the Gulbenkian Museum and the Campo Pequeno bullring. The Cardinal met the procession at the door and inside delivered an address welcoming the Queen of Portugal to the Capital. For the first time the doves left the statue together, flew over to where the Cardinal stood and remained there looking at him and listening to his words as if they understood them. After the welcoming ceremony the birds enjoyed the freedom of the church. Mostly they were to be found on the platform but it wasn't unusual for worshippers to find them flying between their nest of flowers and the patriarchal throne. During the distribution of Holy Communion on 7th December one flew to the crown on the head of the statue and perched there with its wings extended until the last recipient had taken the Sacrament. The other two flew to the top of the ceiling during this time and could not be seen.

At ten o'clock that same evening the three-mile

procession from the church of Our Lady of Fatima to the cathedral began. As the platform was about to be lifted onto the shoulders of the men, two of the doves flew to the edge of a stained glass window which surrounds the Throne of Exposition and poised there, their heads turned towards the departing statue. The third dove remained among the flowers at Our Lady's feet. Outside it was raining heavily but when the statue emerged from the church the rain stopped, the clouds rolled back and the moon appeared.

Along the route most of the population of the city lined the streets, strewing flowers, singing hymns, letting off fireworks and bearing candles. The two doves from the stained-glass window rejoined their companion early in the procession and all three remained with the statue till it reached the cathedral, around 1.00 a.m. At the doors one of the doves suddenly left the platform and flew up to the topmost pinnacle of the ancient *Sé* where it perched, according to witnesses, for at least an hour. Two doves remained with the statue during its night-long vigil in the cathedral, the Pontifical High Mass for the feast of the Immaculate Conception the following day, the solemn *Te Deum* and the renewal of the Act of Consecration of Portugal to the Immaculate Conception. Only one dove, however, was reported to have been with the statue when it was taken from the cathedral to the Praça do Comércio, transferred to a fishing boat, and taken across the Tagus on its long way around back to Fatima. After that reports vary. Some say that one dove was with the statue, and photographed, in

Setúbal on 13th December. The press reported 'doves' with it in Entrocamento on 22nd. The procession arrived back in Fatima on Christmas Eve.

For a long time a cote was kept beneath the eaves of the Capela das Aparições and still today there is always a dove colony in the Santuário though one of the Servitas assures me that there are no cotes now, that the doves, with some pigeon cousins, which perch above the colonnade and invariably attend the 11.00 Recinto Mass in summer, live wild.

It is non-productive to argue whether this presence of the doves during the triumphal procession of the statue of Our Lady of Fatima was the result of divine direction or not. Believers will want to think it was, non-believers that it wasn't. One way or the other it was a phenomenon and, as Fr. Thomas McGlynn OP, the sculptor of the statue of the Immaculate Heart in the niche in the Fatima Basilica façade, pointed out, even unbelievers must admit that Dona Maria Emilia Martins Campos of Bombarral got a great bargain for her seventy-eight escudos.

Peripheral Attractions

Some of the establishments mentioned in this section are privately owned and operated and have no affiliation with the Sanctuary. Admission prices have been omitted because they are subject to fluctuation.

The Museum of Sacred Art and Ethnology
(*Museu de Arte Sacra e Etnologia*)

A number of peripheral attractions have built up around the shrine, some of religious interest, others not. Foremost among them is the Museum of Sacred Art and Ethnology on the Rua Francisco Marto. The Museum is part of the Allamano Missionary Centre run by the Consolata Fathers. Blessed Joseph Allamano, a Diocesan priest from Turin in Italy, founded the Consolata Society for Foreign Missions in 1901. The Fathers have been in Fatima since 1943.

The Centre encompasses three sectors:

1. The chapel, auditorium and meeting rooms.
2. Administration rooms and offices of the Mission's magazine, *Fátima Missionária*.
3. The Museum of Sacred Art and Ethnology. (*Museu de Arte Sacra e Etnologia*).

The museum, the overall theme of which is Christ in Art and in the World, has four exhibiting rooms called Nativity, Passion, Mission and Meeting of Cultures.

1. *Nativity.* Apart from some classical pictures by Portuguese masters, the room contains a collection of Portuguese nativity-related images collected from different periods. The Infants and cribs displayed have been formed from materials ranging from wood, clay, wax and cork to metal, porcelain and ivory. The variety is intriguing and satisfying. Some representations correspond to popular traditions and devotions of the areas of origin – the Child Jesus with a top hat, Jesus Shepherd, the Child as priest, bishop and knight complete with boots, spurs and cloak. And don't miss the display case showing nativity-orientated postage stamps from around the world.

2. *Passion.* In this room there is a wide range of crucifixes and Calvary scenes in a variety of mediums from Portugal itself and from its former territories in Africa, India and Brazil. The outstanding piece is a 1929 *Pieta* by José Thedim, the sculptor of the original Fatima statue which stands in the Capelinha. It is life-size and life-like and it would be an insensitive person indeed who could pass by it without being moved. Here too is another case of postage stamps, this time Passion focused.

3. *The Mission Room* traces the Portuguese Missionary activity that followed the great discoveries of the fifteenth and sixteenth centuries.

4. *The Meeting of Cultures Room* houses an ethnological exhibition. The artifacts here illustrate the life and customs of peoples evangelised by the missionaries – ethnic groups from Kenya, Mozambique, Angola, Zaire, Guiana, the Amazon Basin and Macau.

A visit to this excellent museum cannot be missed. It is appropriate that it is in Fatima, but in whatever town it had been placed, a visit would have repaid the trouble of a detour many times over.

Hours: April–October   10.00–19.00
       Nov.–March   12.00–17.00
       Closed on Monday.

The Museum House of Aljustrel

Situated at the central intersection of Aljustrel, next door to Lucia's house, this is a compact and delightfully arranged display of how the village folk lived at the beginning of the twentieth century – and indeed, probably for long before and even for some time after. Whoever is responsible for bringing this authentic encounter with the past into being in this locale deserves our unstinted accolade. The wooden farm tools and the holy picture table in the parlour were my personal favourites. Don't miss it.

Hours: Check with Information office in the courtyard of Lucia's house.

The Wax Museum (*Museu de Cera de Fátima*)

Situated in an arcade off the Rua Jacinta Marto this is a gallery of thirty wax tableaux showing the story of the Apparitions and later Papal visits to the shrine.

Hours: 10.00–18.30 (Longer during summer, weekends and holidays.)

Apparitions Museum (*Museu Aparições*)

A series of tableaux showing aspects of the apparitions. Visually effective for young children. It is in a basement arcade off the Rua Jacinta Marto. Open daily.

The Story of the Apparitions (*A História das Apparicões*)

A theatre-based display using advanced technology on a very, very wide screen. It takes the form of a documentary of the apparitions of Our Lady and of the angel of Peace, the vision of hell, the miracle of the sun etc. It was previously called *Fatima Fantastica*. The new name is more indicative of the quality on offer. The Bishop of Leiria/Fatima is said to have been present at a performance and endorsed it. Even at only twenty minutes running time it is good value for the money. The very modern facility is situated downstairs in the Fatima Shopping Centre on the Rua

Jacinta Marto. Performances run between 10.00 and 19.00 daily.

(There are reductions for block bookings.)

The Shrine of Our Lady of Ortiga

A couple of kilometres east of the Fatima parish church is the church and shrine of Our Lady of Ortiga. As the site of a much earlier apparition of the Blessed Virgin Ortiga repays a visit. It was shown Papal favour long before the Fatima visions when, in 1801, Pope Pius VII granted a Jubilee indulgence to those who visited it on each First Sunday in July.

The story goes that in some time long past, a shepherd girl who was dumb in the sense that she had no power of speech, was pasturing her flocks on the Ortiga mount when Our Lady appeared to her and asked for a sheep. The girl was so amazed that her tongue was loosened. Dutifully she replied that she could not give a sheep without first asking her father. She ran to her home, which was called *Casal de Santa Maria*, St Mary's Farm, and asked her father if she could give Our Lady a sheep. Her father was so surprised to hear his daughter talking that he told her to give the Lady whatever She asked for.

When the shepherd girl returned to speak to Our Lady She asked for a chapel to be built at Ortiga. Then She disappeared. When the father came to the place later he found a statue standing on a stone among the nettles on the hill-top. He took the statue back to the farm but the following morning it had gone. A search revealed that it was back on its stone among the nettles. This was taken as a sign that the spot was to be the site of the chapel, so one was built there. Over the centuries it was enlarged and refurbished until we have the small but beautifully proportioned place of worship that stands there now.

The bandstand and the two nearby windmills, one old and one new (1997) are of interest.

Ortiga is the Portuguese word for nettle.

Mini-Train
This Italian-built motor vehicle with articulated open carriages runs from both sides of the Sanctuary to the South Roundabout, on to Aljustrel, to Fátima parish church and back. Passengers can hop off at the various stops and board the next train passing along after they have visited the sites along the way.
Summer months only.

Cinema
There is a cinema in the Fátima Shopping Centre (the same well-appointed auditorium as is used for the *History of the Apparitions* show). It screens the latest films at 21.00 each evening and has matinees on Sundays. The films are changed each Friday. As is to be expected they are often at variance with the spirit of the shrine.

Restaurants and cafes
There are many very fine restaurants on both sides of the Sanctuary. On Rua Jacinta Marto perhaps the most popular, because the most central, is the *Panorama* on the first floor with its windows over-

looking the Praça São José. The *Rosmaninho* Cafe on the Rua Francisco Marto side (No. 70), and the cafeteria of the Hotel *Solar da Marta* next door are particularly popular with English speakers.

For top quality there is the *Tia Alice* (Auntie Alice) in Fatima proper opposite the Fatima parish church. Despite its homely frontage it could hold its own in the middle of London, Paris or New York for decor, service, food and general excellence. Also worth a visit is the *Truão* (Court Jester) in Boleiros about 6 kilometres along the Minde road. (You might recall it was at the boys from Boleiros that Francisco threw stones, a misdeed that Jacinta reminded him of before his first, and last, confession on his deathbed.) The building is an old olive-crushing mill and the adaptation to restaurant, banquet rooms etc is a true work of art. If you are there and it is not busy ask the waiter to show you the room with the great crushing stone and the banqueting hall and gallery.

The restaurant at the Estalagem *D. Gonçalo*, in Rua Jacinta Marto, just off the North Rotunda, has a well deserved reputation for excellence. A genuine five-star establishment where the service is impeccable.

A short distance from Fatima
Not far from Fatima are various sites of more interest to the tourist than the pilgrim. Notable among them are:

1. Ourém Castle is worth a visit if one has the leisure.

The view alone is worth the price of a taxi for a small party.

2. The Caves (*Grutas*) – There are a number of these in the hills to the South West of Fatima. The nearest is about 2 kms from the North Roundabout – a sprightly walk on a long afternoon. It is well signposted.

3. The Dinosaur's Footprints (*Pegadas Dinossauros*) – They are in a recently discovered quarry about 10kms from Fatima.

4. The monasteries and churches of Batalha and Alcobaça and the Templars' *Convento de Cristo* in Tomar are all worth seeing as mighty monuments to the Ages of Faith.

5. Even farther afield are the almost forgotten island castle of Almoural, the enchanted forest of Buçaco with the atmospheric Carmelite monastery (*Mosteiro dos Carmelítas*) in the middle of it, the churches and castles of Leiria and Coimbra and Santarem. All these sites are worth seeing, but not if they distract from a prayerful pilgrimage.

Further details can be had from the Tourist Information Office (Posto de Turismo), an imposing building on the Avénida José Alves Correia da Silva where it separates the Santário complex from the Paul VI Pastoral Centre. (This is the State run Tourist Office and is not to be confused with the Sanctuary Information Centre which has an office behind the Capelinha, and another at the top of the steps on the main northern exit from the Recinto.)

Familiar Prayers: Portuguese and English

INTRODUCTION

The Shrine of Fatima is in Portugal. It has a very strong Portuguese character and, although Our Lady's message is for all peoples from all countries, it is the Portuguese who have established and fostered the Shrine and continue to maintain it. At any given time probably 90% of the pilgrims worshipping here are Portuguese. As a consequence most of the liturgy and devotions are, as is proper, conducted in Portuguese. (It might be noted though that the *Misa Official* at the *Recinto* altar and the evening Rosary in the *Capelinha* employ a variety of languages.) It is not necessary to know Portuguese (incidentally, the seventh most spoken language in the world, and the most spoken in the Southern Hemisphere) to follow the public prayers; one can follow them quietly in one's own language, or in the heart, but it is not difficult to learn the oft repeated prayers. To be able to join the Portuguese in the Rosary, especially, is to be using the same language that Our Lady used when speaking with Lucia during the apparitions. This, with all one's stumbling and mistakes, is an act of courtesy to the most courteous of created beings.

The Our Father

Our Father   *Pai nosso*

pai has much the same sound as the English 'pie', which, as some wit has observed, gives a whole new dimension to the irreverent adage 'pie in the sky when you die'.

Nosso, like all Portuguese words (except infinitives) not showing an acute elsewhere, takes the accent on the penultimate syllable. *Nos*-u. The final 'o' has a 'u' sound. (Infinitives, however, usually take the accent on the final syllable).

who art in heaven   *que estais no céu*

que is like saying 'kirk' but stopping short at the 'r', it's very lightly, just slide it off the palate.

estais = esh-*tay*-ish. 's', especially at the end of a word, but in the body too, is often pronounced 'sh'.

no = the 'o' has that 'u' sound again.

céu = *say*-oo. Compare with the French 'ciel' and the English celestial.

hallowed be Thy name   *santificado seja o vosso*
                              nome

santificado = san-tif-ee-*car*-doo. This, as in English, is a past participle – sanctified.

seja = *say*-ja. This is the subjunctive of the verb 'to be'

189

i.e. 'Let it be'. The subjunctive is used much more in Portuguese than it is in English.

o = faint 'u' again, O is the masculine definite article 'the'. This, too, is used much more in Portuguese than in English. A strict translation here would be 'the your name' which sounds distinctly odd in English. But it is defining this particular name as opposed to any other. *O João* distinguishes this John from any other John.

vosso = your. *Vos*-u. Pronounced like nosso.

nome = *no*-mer. Name, obviously.

Thy kingdom come   *venha a nos o vosso reino*

venha = subjunctive again – let it come . *Vain*-ya.

a = ah. Here it means 'to' though the same word is also the feminine form of the definite article, 'the'.

nós = as in boss. Means 'us'.

o = 'the' again.

vosso = 'your' again.

reino = kingdom. Ray-*een*-yo.

Thy will be done   *seja feita a vossa vontade*

seja = again 'let it be'

feita = done. *Fay*-ta. The feminine form of the past participle *fazer* = to do. It is feminine because the word *vontade* coming up is feminine.

vossa = your, again, also feminine this time because *vontade* is feminine. In Portuguese, the ending of the

190

pronoun agrees with the thing spoken of, in this case
vontade, the will, not the possessor, in this case God,
who, for grammatical purposes, is masculine.
vontade = the will, the faculty of choice.

on earth as it is in heaven   *assim na terra como no céu*

assim ... como = A-*sing*; as ... as. 'm' at the end of a
Portuguese word is not pronounced 'm' as we
pronounce it. It is a guttural sound. 'ng' is about as
close as we can get to it in print. *como* = *ko*-mo.
na = *nar*. A combintion of *em*, in, and *a*, the feminine
form of the definite article. So it means 'in the'.
terra = earth. Pronounced almost like 'terror'. The
Portuguese roll their 'r's.
no = the 'o' pronounced almost like a soft 'u' again.
The masculine form of na.
em and *o* = 'in the'.
céu, heaven for the second time.

Give us this day our daily bread   *O pão nosso de cada
                                    dia nos dai hoje*

A word for word transliteration here reads: The
bread our of each day us give today.
pão, bread, is pronounced *pow*-ng. 'ão' at the end of
words also uses the guttural 'ng' sound.
cada = *car*-dar, each.
dia = *dee*-ah, day. This word is an oddity because,
although it ends in an 'a' it is gramatically masculine.

191

We are frequently reminded of this in the morning greeting, *bom dia*, 'good day'. (Not *boa dia*, though *tarde* (afternoon) and *noite* (night) are feminine so we get *boa tarde* and *boa noite*.)

dai = *dye*, just like the Welsh name, is the imperative plural (plural for politeness when addressing the Deity) of the verb *dar*, to give.

hoje = *oh*-je. Today. ('h' is never pronounced in Portuguese.)

| forgive us our trespasses | *perdoai-nos as nossas ofensas* |

perdoar means 'to forgive' and here = pur-*doe*-eye, we have the imperative plural again, this time joined to the nos, 'us'.

ofensas = off-*en*-sash; clearly 'offences' supported by *as* (definite article, feminine, plural) and *nossas* ('our' feminine, plural).

| as we forgive | *assim como nós perdoamos* |

assim como, meaning 'as' again, or 'thus like'.

perdoamos = pur-doe-*ar*-mush, is the first person plural of perdoar meaning here, 'we forgive'. The *nós* means 'we' as well. It is used here simply for emphasis.

192

those who have trespassed against us	*a quem nos tem ofendido*

literally = he whom us have offended.

a quem is the Portuguese way of saying 'whom'. There doesn't seem to be any English rhyme or equivalent for *quem*. If you were to use each of the vowels in this sequence – King Kong Kung Kang Keng – then the last one would be about as close as you'd get to it.

Tem = *teng*, on the same principle as *keng*, above, is the third person singular of the verb *ter*, to have.

ofendido = off-end-*ee*-do, the past participle, offended. (Notice how in English we forgive those – plural – who have tresspassed against us, while in Portuguese we forgive the singular – he who has offended.)

and deliver us not into temptation	*e não nos deixeis cair em tentação*

e, and. Don't confuse with *é* = is.

não 'no', or 'not' = Has a *nawng* sound but very light, almost as if you can't be bothered to finish the word.

nos = yet again, is 'us'.

deixeis = day-*shay*-ish, ('x' also takes the 'sh' sound) means you leave, or let. This is the 2nd person plural form of the verb *deixar*. To use the plural form, though speaking to one person is an old fashioned way of showing deference. (The Turkish language still

193

uses it exclusively except to immediate family and
children.)

cair = kay-*ear*, is the infinitive, to fall.

em, as we have seen, is 'in'.

tentação = ten-ta-*sow*-ng. It doesn't take a great intel-
lectual leap to divine the meaning of this word. The
Portuguese here – and don't let us fall into temptation
– must be much nearer Our Saviour's meaning when
he taught us the prayer, than the English version, 'and
lead us not into temptation' which sounds almost blas-
phemous in the active voice.

but deliver us from evil. Amen. *mas livrai-nos do*
                                        mal. Amen.

mas = *mash*, but.

livrai-nos = *leave*-rye-nosh, = the imperative (pl.) of
livrar, to deliver. The nos, of course, is 'us'.

do, like *no*, *do* is a combination word from '*de*'
meaning of and *o* meaning 'the'.

mal = *marl*. Bad or evil.

Amen.   *Amen.*

Amen = the Latin ah-*men* as opposed to the English
A-men.

The Hail Mary

Hail Mary, full of grace,   *Ave-Maria, cheia de graça,*

cheia de graça = *shay*-e-a day *grass*-a

the Lord is with thee   *o Senhor é convosco*

o = the slight 'u' sound again.
Senhor = sen-*yore*, means Lord, (and Mister i.e. Master)
é = 'a' as in Able. It's the 3rd person singular of the verb *ser*, to be.
convosco = con-*voss*-co. With you. (*comigo*, with me; *connosco*, with us etc.)

blessed art thou among   *bendita sois Vós entre as*
women   *mulheres*

bendita = ben-*dee*-ta. Adjective, blessed, hallowed, holy. (In Portuguese the Holy Souls are *Almas benditas*.)
sois Vós = soish *vos*. Archaic way of saying 'you are'.
entre = *eng*-tray
as mulheres = ash mul-*yeah*-raysh. 'as', the (pl) indefinite article again, not used in the English.

195

| and blessed is the fruit of thy womb | *e bendito é o fruto do vosso ventre,* |

By this time the clause should speak for itself. It contains an example of the *e*, and, as well as the *é*, is. It doesn't take a degree in semantics to sort out that *fruto* is fruit and that it is a masculine noun. *ventre*, womb, is pronounced like *entre* above and the phrase *do vosso ventre* transliterates as 'of the your womb'.

| Jesus. | *Jesus.* |

Jesus = *Jay*-zush

| Holy Mary, Mother of God | *Santa Maria, Mãe de Deus,* |

mãe = *my*-ng. Obviously 'mother'.
Deus = *day*-ush.

| pray for us, sinners, | *rogai por nós, pecadores,* |

rogai = *ro*-guy, the imperative of *rogar*, to beseech, or pray.
por nós = poor **nosh**. por is used here in its sense of 'on behalf of'.
pecadores = peck-a-**door**-ash. (This last syllable is as if one has almost said Asia.)
Don't confuse *pecadores*, sinners, with *pescadores*, fishermen.

196

now and at the hour of our death.	*agora e na hora da nossa morte.*

Literally: now and in the hour of the our death.
agora = a-*gore*-ah. Obviously means 'now'.
hora = *or*-ra. The 'h' is never pronounced in Portuguese.
morte = *mort*-e. It's a feminine noun so it takes the feminine *nossa*.

The Glory be to the Father

Glory be to the Father	*Glória ao Pai.*

Glória. In Portuguese the accent is always on the second to last syllable unless an acute indicates otherwise, as here. = *Glore* – ria. (not Glor-*ri*-ah.)

Ao, another combination word – *a* to and *o* the.

and to the Son and to the Holy Spirit	*e ao Filho e ao Espírito Santo;*

by this time there should be no problems. (Note acute in *Espírito*.)

as it was in the beginning,	*como era no princípio,*
is now and ever shall be.	*agora e sempre.*
Amen.	*Amen.*

Literally: as it was in the beginning (note acute), now and always. Amen.

The Sign of the Cross

Em nome do Pai e do Filho e do Espírito Santo. Amen.

Some Interesting Facts Relating to Fatima

During the 1917 apparitions Our Lady confided things to the children that She asked them not to reveal. These have become known as the 'secret' of Fatima. On 17th December 1927 Our Lord appeared to Lucia and told her to make known the first two parts of the secret, which, in fact, comprised the message of Fatima:

1. The vision of hell, the promise to take the children to heaven, the prediction of another war heralded by the lighting up of the sky at night, the destruction of nations, martyrdom of Christians, the sufferings of the Popes, the persecution of the Church and the spread of atheistic Communism.
2. Devotion to the Immaculate Heart of Mary which would, in the end, conquer evil.

The third part of the 'secret' was substantially revealed by Cardinal Sodano after the Papal Mass of Beatification in Fatima on 13th May 2000. It was the Cardinal rather than the Holy Father who made the announcement because the assassination attempt on the Holy Father himself was a part of the prophecy and also, as it was a matter of private revelation, it was more fitting that it was not announced by the Head of the Church. The text of Cardinal Sodano's speech follows:

STATEMENT OF CARDINAL ANGELO SODANO
At the Conclusion of the Holy Father's Mass at Fatima.

'Brothers and Sisters in the Lord!

'At the conclusion of this solemn celebration, I feel bound to offer our beloved Holy Father John Paul II, on behalf of all present, heartfelt good wishes for his approaching eightieth birthday and to thank him for his significant pastoral ministry for the good of all God's Holy Church.

'On the solemn occasion of his visit to Fatima, His Holiness has directed me to make an announcement to you. As you know, the purpose of his visit to Fatima has been to beatify the two 'little shepherds'. Nevertheless he also wishes his pilgrimage to be a renewed gesture of gratitude to Our Lady for Her protection during these years of his papacy. This protection seems also to be linked to the so-called 'third part' of the secret of Fatima. That text contains a prophetic vision similar to those found in Sacred Scripture, which do not describe with photographic clarity the details of future events, but rather synthesize and condense against a unified background events spread out over time in a succession and duration which are not specified. As a result, the text must be interpreted *in a symbolic key*.

'The vision of Fatima concerns above all the war waged by atheist systems against the Church and Christians, and it describes the immense suffering endured by the witnesses to the faith in the last century of the second millennium. It is an interminable *Way of the Cross* led by the Popes of the twentieth century.

'According to the interpretation of the "little shepherds", which was also recently confirmed by Sister Lucia, the "Bishop clothed in white" who prays for all the faithful is the Pope. As he makes his way with great effort towards the Cross amid the corpses of those who were martyred (bishops, priests, men and women religious and many lay persons), he too falls to the ground, apparently dead, under a burst of gunfire. After the assassination attempt of 13th May 1981, it appeared evident to His Holiness that it was "a motherly hand which guided the bullet's path," enabling the "dying Pope" to halt "at the threshold of Death" (Pope John Paul II. *Meditation with the Italian Bishops from the Policlinico Gemelli, Insegnamenti*, vol. XVII/1, 1994, p. 1061). On the occasion of a visit to Rome by the then Bishop of Leiria-Fatima, the Pope decided to give him the bullet which had remained in the jeep after the assassination attempt, so that it might be kept in the Shrine. At the behest of the Bishop, the bullet was later set in the crown of the statue of Our Lady of Fatima.

'The successive events of 1989 led, both in the Soviet Union and in a number of countries of Eastern

Europe, to the fall of the Communist regime which promoted atheism. For this too His Holiness offers heartfelt thanks to the Most Holy Virgin. In other parts of the world, however, attacks against the Church and against Christians, together with the burden of suffering which they involve, tragically continue. Even if the events to which the third part of the Secret of Fatima refers now seem part of the past, Our Lady's call to conversion and penance, issued at the beginning of the twentieth century, remains timely and urgent today. 'The Lady of the message seems to read the signs of the times – the signs of our time – with special insight ... The insistent invitation of Mary Most Holy to penance is nothing but the manifestation of Her maternal concern for the fate of the human family, in need of conversion and forgiveness' (Pope John Paul II, Message for the 1997 World Day of the Sick, No.1, in *Insegnamenti*, vol. XIX/2, 1996, p. 561).

'In order that the faithful may better receive the message of Our Lady of Fatima, the Pope has charged the Congregation for the Doctrine of the Faith with making public the third part of the secret, after the preparation of an appropriate commentary.

'Let us thank Our Lady of Fatima for her protection. To her maternal intercession let us entrust the Church of the Third Millennium.

Sub tuum praesidium confugimus, Sancta Dei Genetrix!'

The actual text of the 'third secret' can be found in the report on the July 1917 apparition on page 9.

At the exact hour that Our Lady was appearing to Lucia, Francisco and Jacinta in Cova da Iria on 13th May 1917 Eugenio Pacelli, (1876–1958) the future Pope Pius XII, was being consecrated a bishop in Rome. After being elected to St Peter's Chair in 1939 he was known as the Pope of Fatima.

Julian of Norwich, the great fourteenth-century English mystic received her sixteen showings, or visions of Christ and many things pertaining to him, on the same day as the first of the Fatima apparitions, 13th May, albeit five hundred and forty-four years before in 1373.

This revelation was made to a simple, unlettered creature, living in this mortal flesh, the year of Our Lord one thousand, three hundred and seventy three, on the thirteenth day of May (*The Showings of Julian of Norwich*, Classics of Western Spirituality, Ch. 2, p. 177).

A musical called *Fatima* by a one-time nurse and later graduate of New York University's School for Writing Musical Theatre, Barbara Oleynick, has had initial readings in the University's Black Box theatre. With the proper backing it looks set to make it to Broadway. One thing that Ms Oleynick has been firm about is adherence to the historical facts, and changing nothing for dramatic effect, which bodes well for the production.

When the atomic bomb destroyed Hiroshima in 1945, eight men living near the blinding centre of the nuclear flash miraculously survived the searing hurricane of blast and gamma rays, while everyone within a mile radius perished and others residing further afield continue to die from the lethal effects of radiation. For over thirty years more than two hundred scientists have examined these eight men, trying in vain to determine what could have preserved them from incineration. One of the survivors, Fr. Ha. Shiffner, SJ, gave the dramatic answer on TV in America: *In that house, we were living the message of Fatima.* (*Fatima, The Great Sign* by Francis Johnston).

Lucia herself never saw the Miracle of the Sun. In 1947 she told Fr. Thomas McGlynn OP that Our Lady appeared as usual and that at a certain point She turned Her hand towards the sun. Lucia exclaimed, 'Look at the sun,' though she had no memory of making any utterance. 'Then appeared at Her side, first, St Joseph and the Child Jesus; then Our Lord;

then there were changes of light in which Our Lady took on different aspects – Our Lady of Sorrows and Our Lady of Mount Carmel. While this was going on the people cried out that they saw the phenomenon in the sun; I myself did not see it.'

Many countries, organisations and individuals give gifts to the Shrine, as we have seen, but this is not all one-sided. The Bishops of Leiria-Fatima sometimes give gifts of special statues of Our Lady of Fatima as tokens of appreciation. In 1950 the Bishop had a statue of Our Lady hand-carved and sent to the national offices of the Blue Army in Washington, New Jersey in acknowledgement of the work done by that organisation in the United States.

The Feast of Our Lady of the Rosary of Fatima was instituted by Pope John XXIII on 13th December 1962. The feast day, naturally enough, was designated as 13th May. On the first celebration of the feast Cardinal Larraona, the Papal Legate at Fatima, directed his homily to the world's priests in which he said, 'There never has been a supernatural manifestation of Our Lady of such rich spiritual content as that of Fatima, nor has any recognised apparition given us a message so clear, so maternal, so profound. Live it and cause it to be lived!'

The tree on which the Blessed Virgin stood on the five occasions that She appeared to the children at the Cova da Iria was a type of oak – *Quercus Ilex*, called Azinheira in Portuguese and, variously, Holm or Holly or Flex or Evergreen oak in English. It is common in the Mediterranean area and a mature tree can grow up to twenty metres. The actual tree of the apparitions was only a shrub, about a metre high. During that summer of 1917 it was stripped bare of leaves and branches by souvenir seekers till it was no more than a stump. Maria Carreira decorated it with ribbons and flowers for the later apparitions. It was fenced off after the apparitions in the hope that it might resprout but it didn't and was eventually covered with a column, the forerunner of the one on which the statue of the Virgin now stands.

The first church outside Portugal to be named in honour of Our Lady of Fatima is in Great Britain, in Bala in North Wales, in fact. In 1937 a local priest was having great difficulty in finding a property to use as a church. He prayed to Our Lady of Fatima and at once he was provided with a derelict property that had been the local fish and chip shop. The building was duly converted to a place of worship and in 1948 it was consecrated with great ceremony in the presence of the Portuguese Vice-Consul and many prominent British Catholics. A special statue was carved in the Cova da Iria and transported to Bala in an open-topped car. On its arrival in Liverpool the car was decorated with flags of the Pope, Portugal and Wales and was accompanied on the last leg of its journey by coachloads of worshippers. On 21st May 1960 the statue was crowned with a jewelled crown by Bishop John Murphy of Shrewsbury. The tiny church can only hold twenty people so on evenings when the number of pilgrims exceeds the capacity of the building it is said that a spontaneous candle-lit procession is held.

Domus Pacis: The Blue Army Headquarters. It is not within the scope of this handbook, which is centred on the Shrine of Fatima, to include information on the privately-owned hotels, *residenciales*, pensions and guest houses which abound in the town. However, the great onion dome, which dominates the skyline to the east, deserves some explanation because of its imposing presence and because it is owned by the American-founded Blue Army of Our Lady of Fatima. It is called Domus Pacis, the House of Peace. The site was actually purchased in 1950 by Monsignor Harold Colgan, the founder of the Blue Army (*Exercito Azul* in Portuguese). The location was suggested by Teresa dos Santos Pereira of Lomba, a sister of the seer Lucia. At the time the new Basilica of Our Lady of the

Rosary, a hundred metres or so to the west, was still four years off completion. It was to be a multi-purpose building. Accommodation for pilgrims to Fatima was a priority – at the time the only other pilgrimage house in the town was the Hotel Pax run by the Consolata Fathers – but it was also to be an educational facility to provide formation in the Fatima message, a centre for the international secreteriat, and a base of operations for propagating the Fatima message inside Russia. The cornerstone was laid in May 1953. An early estimate for the work was $75,000. By 1955 this had escalated to $500,000. By the summer of 1955 lack of funds caused the work to be halted. In the States a big drive for cash to complete the project was set up. Monsignor Harold Colgan led the way as much by deeds as by words. He sold his car and eschewed all but the necessities of life until the work was completed. Domus Pacis was blessed by Cardinal Eugene Tisserant, Head of the Congregation for the Oriental Church, on 12th October 1956, but the building wasn't actually occupied until 1958.

For many years Domus Pacis housed the famous thirteenth–fourteenth century Icon of Kazan in its upper floor Byzantine chapel. This icon of Our Lady and the Child Jesus is of great historical significance for the Russian people. To escape desecration it was smuggled out of Russia after the Bolshevik revolution. The Blue Army was able to acquire it and were safeguarding it until Our Lady's work in Russia created a climate where it could be happily returned. In 1993 it was transferred to the Vatican for security reasons and negotiations are already underway to return it to its rightful home.

For thirty years Domus Pacis flourished and played host to many thousands of pilgrims who have refreshed at the wellsprings of Mary and returned to their homes eager to spread her message.

With its accommodation facilities it is still popular with Americans. But the real core of its activity is in its chapels where the Blessed Eucharist is reserved. Pilgrims might note the four foot high statue of Our Lady in the Latin Chapel and the statue of the Sacred Heart at its entrance. These images were both present in the Dorothean convent in Tuy, Spain when Our Lady appeared to Lucia to ask for the consecration of Russia to her Immaculate Heart. It is fitting that they should now be here, under the onion dome. Around 1910 two young academics shared a flat in the university city of Coimbra. One, a newly ordained priest, lectured in history. The other, whose discipline was economics, was in minor orders but had decided not to become a priest. The history lecturer went on to become Cardinal Cerejeira, the Patriarch of Lisbon. The economist was Antonio de Oliveira Salazar who was to rule Portugal for forty years. Both were stalwart champions of Fatima.

Blessed Padre Pio received the stigmata in 1918 – the year after Our Lady appeared at Fatima. He was beatified just one year before Francisco and Jacinta Marto. On 13th February 1961 the Bishop of Leiria blessed a statue of Our Lady of Fatima which was a private gift from a Portuguese family to Padre Pio. It is possibly the statue which currently stands in the vestry of the church at San Giovani Rotondo.

Pope Pius XII was known as the Pope of Fatima. He is recorded as having said, 'Fatima is the summation of my thinking.' And, 'The time for doubting Fatima is past; it is now time for action'. At the closing of the extended 1950 Holy Year, which took place in Fatima on 13th October 1951, Cardinal Tedeschini, the Papal Legate, revealed to an immense crowd that that Pius XII had seen a repetition of the 1917 solar miracle in the Vatican Gardens on the eve of 1st November 1950, the day of the promulgation of the dogma of the Corporal Assumption of the Blessed Virgin Mary.

On the feast of St Michael, 29th September 1916, a Eucharistic procession was held in the parish of Juncal, about 25 km north east of Fatima. The church there is named for St Michael the Archangel and the event was a tradition. After the procession the parish priest, Father Luis da Costa Carvalho, placed the large, consecrated Host from the monstrance in the tabernacle. In the same tabernacle he, somewhat unconventionally, always kept the chalice which he used for daily Mass. When this was done he locked the tabernacle with the only key.

The following day when Father Carvalho unlocked the tabernacle to prepare for Mass, the large Host was not there. Furthermore the chalice was not in its customary position, and there were fresh wine stains (precious blood!) on the material lining of the tabernacle.

Father Carvalho told his curate and several parishioners of the inexplicable happening but the fate of the Host and the presence of the stains remained a mystery to him right up till he died twenty years later on 3rd September 1937.

In November that same year Lucia revealed the appearance of the angel with a Host and chalice at Cabeço before the Marian apparitions. Knowing that only an ordained priest can consecrate the bread and wine so that they become the Body and Blood of Jesus Christ, and therefore that the angel must have obtained the Host from somewhere, it is not too fanciful to suppose that the Juncal Host and chalice were taken by the angel for that purpose, and the chalice replaced.

Many authorities consider that the angel who called himself the Angel of Peace and the Angel of Portugal was, in fact, St Michael and that he took the Host and borrowed the chalice from his own church. Above the entrance to this building is a massive sculpture in stone of St Michael (1780) and beneath it, as if to prefigure the Fatima communions, is a chalice surrounded by angels.

The *Miraculada*, that is, the person whose cure was accepted by Rome as a miracle wrought through the intercession of Francisco and Jacinta and which opened the way for their beatification, was a paralysed lady from the city of Leiria, Maria Emília dos Santos (no relation to Lucia). After the miracle Maria Emília lived a normal life until it was found, in May 2000, just after the beatifications, that she had leukemia. She died at the end of November. She was seventy years of age.

The lamps hanging from the ceiling of the colonnade are five-sided. Each of the five corners is decorated with a ten-beaded upright. The pending piece which supports the lamps from the ceiling has two large beads enclosing three smaller ones. Each lamp is, in fact, a Rosary.

Quick Biographies

WHO'S WHO IN THE FATIMA STORY

The pilgrim who hasn't made a detailed study of the Fatima story can be excused for being confused with the many different names he is confronted with, particularly as these names are mostly in a language foreign to him. This section lists the more commonly encountered names along with some dates and biographical details. The length of the entry does not necessarily reflect the importance of the part played by that person.

Bishops of Leiria–Fátima: The diocese of Leiria was originally created at the request of the Portuguese king, Dom João 111 by Pope Paul III, with the Bull *Pro Excellenti* on 22nd May 1545. The See was disestablished for political reasons on 4th September 1882 but was restored – the timing, though felicitous, was not initiated or influenced by the apparitions – on 17th January 1918 with the Bull *Quo Vehementis* by Benedict XV. Between 1882 and 1918 the responsibility for the territory was divided between the dioceses of Coimbra and Lisbon. A decree of the Sacred

Congregation of Bishops on 13th May 1984, confirmed by the Papal Bull *Qua Pietate* in the same year, gave the diocese the official title Leiria-Fátima.

Since the 1918 restoration the Bishops of the diocese have been:

D. José Alves Correia da Silva (1872–1957) Bishop of Leiria-Fátima 1920–1957.

D. João Pereira Venâncio (1904–1972) Bishop of Leiria-Fátima 1958–1972.

D. Alberto Cosme do Amaral (b. 1916) Bishop of Leiria-Fátima 1972–1993.

D. Serafim de Sousa Ferreira e Silva (b. 1930) Bishop of Leiria-Fátima 1993.

Cerejeira, Cardinal: Cardinal Patriarch of Lisbon during the crucial years of the shrine's development.

Colgan, Monsignor Harold (d. 1972): In 1946, while Parish priest of St Mary's, Plainfield, New Jersey USA, Father Colgan lay dying of a heart ailment. He made a vow to the Blessed Virgin that if She would cure him he would devote the rest of his life to propagating the message of Fatima. Days later he walked out of the hospital in perfect physical condition and the establishment of the Blue Army of Our Lady of Fatima was the beginning of the fulfilment of his promise. After twenty-five years of indefatigable work which saw the Blue Army become an international organisation Monsignor Colgan died and is buried in the crypt beneath the Holy House Chapel in the grounds of the National Blue Army Shrine of the Immaculate Heart of Mary in Washington, New Jersey.

Fischer, Father Doctor Ludwig (1890–1957): Apostle and messenger of Fatima. He was a teacher at the University of Bamberg in 1920. He made his first pilgrimage to Fatima in 1929. He founded the magazine *Bote von Fatima* (Fatima Messenger) in 1931 and a Fatima publishing house in 1932. In 1935 he presided over the translation of the body of Jacinta from the crypt in Ourém to Fatima when it was found to be incorrupt. A plaque commemorating him is to be found next to the Berlin Wall.

Formigão, Canon Doctor Manuel Nunes (1883–1958): Ordained in Rome in 1908. He was a canon and a professor of theology at Santarem at the time of the apparitions and among the first priests to be present at any of them. That was on 13th September 1917. On 27th of that same September he interrogated each of the three seers separately and has left a lengthy record of these important interviews. It was he, along with the doctor, who advised Jacinta's parents that she should be sent to the hospital in Lisbon where she died. He became one of the leading protagonists of the cult of Fatima in Portugal. In 1926 he founded the Sisters of Reparation of Our Lady of Sorrows who, among other things, keep perpetual vigil before the Blessed Sacrament in the Chapel of

Perpetual Adoration. He is commemorated in a series of black marble tablets alongside the repository of the section of the Berlin Wall.

Francisco Marto (11.6.08–4.4.19): Declared venerable 13.5.89. Beatified 13.5.2000. One of the three seers. He was one year and ten months older than his sister Jacinta and one year and almost three months younger than his cousin Lucia. He was the first to die, just short of two years after the first apparition. He made his First Communion (apart from the Precious Blood received at the hands of the angel in Cabeço before the apparitions) two days before he died. He was buried in the cemetery of the Fatima church with no other memorial than a simple cross set up by Lucia. On 12th September 1935 his bones were exhumed and placed in a new tomb especially built for him and Jacinta. On 13th March 1952 his remains were again exhumed and transferred to a grave on the south side of the nave in the Basilica. The headstone reads, in part, HERE LIE THE MORTAL REMAINS OF FRANCISCO MARTO TO WHOM OUR LADY APPEARED.

Godinho, Mother: The admirable nun who ran the orphanage in the *Rua da Estrela* between the Rato and Lapa districts of Lisbon. The orphanage had a choir which adjoined the Chapel of Miracles near the Basilica of Estrela. It was here that Jacinta stayed before going to the Estefánia Hospital where she died. It was here also that she received the Blessed

Sacrament. The children called Mother Godinho *Madrinha*, godmother. (The orphanage is now a Poor Clare convent though Jacinta's rooms are open to the faithful, as is the Chapel of Miracles.)

Jacinta Marto (11.3.10–20.2.20): Declared venerable 13th May 1989. Beatified 13th May 2000. The youngest of the three seers. She was the sister of Francisco and the cousin of Lucia. She died two years and nine months after the first apparition of the Blessed Virgin. Her death occurred in bed no. 60 of ward no. 1 (the children's ward) of Lisbon's Dona Estafánia Hospital ten days after an operation to remove her seventh and eighth left ribs and drain off purulent matter – an ordeal she had undergone without anaesthetic. She died alone, as Our Lady had told her she would. Our Lady had also told her that she would return to Fatima after her death. She was to have been buried in one of the Lisbon cemetcrics the following day but in fact her body lay in the church of the Holy Angels for four days. (The undertaker, Antonio Almeida, later wrote: 'I have seen many corpses, large and small, but I have never seen anything like that. The beautiful perfume which the body exhaled could not be explained naturally and the hardest sceptic could not doubt it. One remembers the smell which so often makes it repugnant to remain near a corpse and yet this child had been dead three days and a half and the smell of her body was like a bouquet of flowers ...') The body was sealed in a lead coffin and taken by train to Fatima where it was buried in the vault of Baron Alvaiázere in Villa Nova de Ourem. In 1935 the Baron gave up the remains (which, he affirmed, had brought so many graces on his family), when the Bishop wanted the bodies of the two seers to be together in a Fatima tomb. During the transition the body was found to be incorrupt. On 1st May 1951 the remains were transferred to the Basilica to a grave on the left of the nave. Beside her another grave awaits the interment of the body of her cousin, Lucia, who, at the time of writing this, is still alive.

Lucia dos Santos (b. 22.3.07.): The eldest of the three seers and the only one who actually spoke to Our Lady. On 16th June 1921, at the instigation of the Bishop who acted for her own protection with her and her mother's consent, she left Fatima to enter, under the assumed name Maria das Dores, the college of the Dorotheas in Vilar, near Oporto. She had just turned fourteen. She later joined the Dorothean congregation spending time in their house in Tuy and Pontevedra in Spain and then back to the Oporto area. As a Dorothean she had the name Sister Maria Lucia de Jesus though it appears she was known as Irma Dores. On 25th December 1948 she transferred from the Dorotheans to the enclosed Carmelites in Coimbra where she is Sister Mary of the Immaculate Heart. She had further visions of Our Lady in December 1925, February 1926 and June 1929 in Spain. She returned to Fatima as a Dorothean to identify sites

218

associated with the apparitions, and in 1967, and at the invitation of Pope John Paul II when he visited in 1982 to thank Our Lady for sparing his life from the attack of the assassin Ali Agci in St Peter's Square on Fatima Day the previous year, and again in 1991 for the tenth anniversary of that attack. She was ninety-four in March 2001.

Maria Carreira: also known as Maria da Capelinha. She was from Moita, the village on the hill to the north of Cova da Iria. She was bed-ridden and hadn't left her house for many years. She had a couple of daughters and a crippled son John. (It was this John of whom Our Lady spoke during the July apparitions when She said **'I will neither cure him nor change his state of poverty; let him say the Rosary daily with all his family.'** But She did provide him with a means of livelihood because he was to be the sacristan of the shrine for fifty years.) When told of the first apparition by her husband she said she would leave her bed and go there, which she did. Thereafter she kept the site clean and provided table and candles etc. Indeed, she kept on looking after it for the rest of her life.

THE SAINTS OF THE STATUES

There are seventeen statues representing eighteen saints. (John Bosco and his pupil Dominic Savio are sculpted together.) There are five Portuguese, five

French, four Italians, three Spaniards and one English. Two are women, fifteen are men and one is a boy. All but one (Blessed Nuno) are canonised.

The Major Statues

Saint John of God (1495–1550)

This colourful character was born in Montemor-a-Novo, amid, it is said, many wonders. At eight he followed a Spanish priest to Spain and was left with a shepherd. Grown to manhood he left the shepherd, who was all for marrying John to his daughter, and joined the army of Charles V. Thereafter he seems to have been in various parts of Europe and North Africa. In Gibraltar he is said to have had a vision of the Child Jesus who gave him the name, John of God. He repented of his ways but his change of heart was manifested in such extreme forms that he was confined for a time as a lunatic.

In 1537 he determined to devote himself to the sick and destitute, while earning his living as a wood merchant. With the help of the Archbishop of Granada he took a house and for ten years gave shelter and care to those in need. It was not until after his death that his followers were organised into an order of hospitallers, the Brothers of St John of God, whose work has spread far and wide. They have a house in the Rua São João de Deus behind the Basilica. His feast is on 8th March.

Saint John de Brito (1647–1693)

A Portuguese Jesuit from Lisbon, he went to Madras, India, as a Missionary in 1673. He adapted himself as far as possible to the manners and customs of the people among whom he lived, but the success of his mission eventually led to his death. A convert to Christianity, having been a polygamist, put away his extra wives. One of them complained to her uncle the Rajah of Marava. The Rajah thereupon began a persecution of Christians and John de Brito was beheaded for subverting the religion of the country. A moving letter he wrote to his fellow missionaries on the eve of his execution is extant. His feast is on 4th February.

Saint Anthony of Lisbon (c. 1195–1231)

Better known as Anthony of Padua outside Portugal this saint is unique in being canonised a year after he died at the age of thirty-six. He was born in Lisbon and, at the age of twenty-five, was an Augustinian canon studying in Coimbra, when he suddenly joined the newly formed Franciscan Friars who sent him to work among the Moslems in Morocco. His health failed and he returned to Europe, specifically Italy. He was in a hermitage but soon discovered that he had an unusual gift for preaching. This he exercised to the full for the next nine years as well as teaching and filling other posts of his order in Italy and France. He died in Padua and is buried there.

The statues of St Anthony showing him as a rather soft young man carrying the child Jesus and a lily, do not do him justice. He was strong and fearless, merciless towards oppressors of the defenceless and towards ill-living clergy. In his lifetime he was called the *Hammer of Heretics*. The text of many of his sermons has survived and because of these and his reputation as a biblical scholar the Church reckons him among her doctors. His feast is on 13th June.

Blessed Nuno of St Mary (1360–1431)

Nuno Álvares de Pereira. He was an outstanding military leader, known as the Holy Constable, whose victory over Castilian forces in the historic Battle of Aljubarrota on 14th August 1385 assured Portugal's independence. He continued to fight against the Castilians until the final peace of 1411. He then lent his support to the expedition that captured Sueta in northern Morocco from the Moors.

Nuno, who had had a Carmelite house built in Lisbon in fulfilment of a vow, entered it himself as Friar Nuno de Santa Maria in 1423. He was beatified by Pope Benedict XV on 23rd Jan 1918. His feast day is kept on 6th November.

The Smaller Statues

Saint Teresa of Ávila (1515–1582)

The great Carmelite doesn't need an introduction. In 1970, along with St Catherine of Sienna, she was declared a Doctor of the Church – the first women ever to be so honoured. She was born Teresa de Cepeday Ahumada. She was from a good family, was naturally gifted and had a lively disposition. She became a nun in the Carmelite Convent of the Incarnation in her native Ávila when she was twenty – with determination, it is said, but without enthusiasm. But she persevered and reached a very high state of prayer.

It wasn't until she was in her mid-forties that she knew her calling was to found a convent under the original, strict form of the Carmelite rule. She suffered the almost obligatory setbacks but finally opened the first house of the reform at St Joseph's in Ávila in 1562. In 1568 she helped reform the male Carmelites. During the next twenty years Teresa travelled up and down Spain founding convents, seventeen in all. The communities were to be small, poor, strictly enclosed and highly disciplined with daily mental prayer a priority. Under her influence the reform spread to the men of the order, outstanding among their leaders being St John of the Cross. Her books, *Life, Way of Perfection, Book of Foundations* and *The Interior Castle* are themselves classics among the classics of spirituality.

Saint Francis de Sales (1567–1622)

This much loved saint was a Savoyard, born in the Château de Sales at Thorens near Annecy. In spite of family opposition he was ordained priest in 1593 and his first mission was to preach to his local people who had gone over to Calvinism. The spirit with which he approached them is shown by his own saying that whoever preaches with love preaches effectively. By the end of four years most had returned to the Roman Catholic Church. In 1602 he was made Bishop of Geneva. Soon after he met Jane Francis de Chantal and with her founded the Visitation order. It was at one of the Visitation convents that Francis died, still in his mid-fifties.

His two great works are the *Introduction to the Devout Life* and *The Love of God*. The Introduction was unusual in its day in that it wasn't written with Religious under vows in mind. It maps out the path to holiness for everyone from the soldier to the shopkeeper to the housewife. It was appreciated by such diverse characters as King James I of England and John Wesley. He is a Doctor of the Church and the patron of journalists and writers. His feast day is 24th January.

Saint Marcellin de Champagnat (1789–1840)
A Marist priest who founded the Little Brothers of Mary (Marist Brothers), a teaching institute, in Lyons in 1817, approved in 1863. When the religious orders were expelled from France in 1903 the brothers had seven hundred and fifty schools. When the statues in the Santuário were erected Benedict Marcellin Champagnat was still Blessed. He was canonised in Rome on 18th April 1999.

Saint John-Baptiste de La Salle (1651–1719)
He was born in Rheims and held its canonry even as a teenager, long before being ordained. However he abandoned his life of ease to devote himself to the

education of the poor. This led to the formation of the Brothers of the Christian Schools, known now as the de La Salle Brothers. In 1688 he took over a free school in Paris and also introduced Sunday Schools. The exiled Catholic Stuart, King James II of England, invited him to provide education for the sons of the gentry in his entourage. In 1700 he opened a school in Rome. His congregation suffered the usual setbacks that attend any innovative work yet it continued to expand and is still healthy today in all parts of the world, the de La Salle establishments ranging from primary schools to teachers' training and university colleges.

John-Baptiste's book, *The Conduct of Christian Schools*, was a milestone in the schooling of the young with its use of the 'simultaneous method' and its teaching through the mother tongue rather than Latin. Matthew Arnold said of this book that later works on the subject hardly improved on its precepts and had none of its religious feeling. John-Baptiste de La Salle's statue in the Santuário depicts him standing with a pupil. His feast is on 7th April.

Saint Alphonsus Maria de Ligouri (1696–1787)
He came from the Naples area and at first studied law but having lost an important case in 1723 changed careers and studied for the priesthood. Making his mark as a preacher he gathered a group of priests around him which in time became the Congregation of the Most Holy Redeemer – known today as the Redemptorists. In 1748 he published the first version

of his work on moral theology, which became so famous that it somewhat overshadowed his other achievements.

In 1762 an order of the Pope forced Alphonsus to accept a bishopric which he held for thirteen years until he was forced to resign through bad health. In his last years he had to contend with a permanent deformity, attacks on his teaching and troubles among the Redemptorists. Indeed, he died excluded from the congregation he had founded. But if his end seemed a failure on human terms it was the opposite in the ledgers of heaven. He was canonised a mere fifty years after his death and is today considered one of the great lights of the eighteenth century Church. His feast is kept on 1st August.

Saint John Bosco (1815–1888) and *Saint Dominic Savio* (1842–1857)

John Bosco was brought up in peasant conditions in Piedmont by his widowed mother. He was ordained priest in 1841 and worked in a poor suburb of Turin. He had a special talent for getting through to young people and before long he had hundreds attending his chapel and his evening classes. Soon, with his mother as housekeeper, he had opened boarding houses for apprentices, and workshops for teaching occupational skills. These activities grew and led, in 1858, to the foundation of a congregation to carry on the work. He called the congregation Salesian as he wanted it to incorporate the spirit of St Francis de Sales. Later, in 1872, with the help of a peasant woman from near

Genoa, Mary Mazzarello – she was canonised in 1951 – he started a congregation called Daughters of Mary, Help of Christians, to do similar work among girls.

His genius with boys was partly inborn, partly the fruit of experience. He said that he had no formal system of education, that he sought to make things attractive, whether school subjects or religious practice. A large number of seemingly miraculous events, like the multiplication of food, are recorded of John Bosco, many of then very well attested.

One of his protégés was Dominic Savio, whom John Bosco hoped to train as a helper but the boy died when he was not quite fifteen. John Bosco wrote a biography of him. No one doubted Dominic's exceptional holiness but the canonisation in 1954 of one so young was not uncontested. Young martyrs apart, his case was unique, although with the beatification of Francisco and Jacinta Marto, and probable canonisation before too long, he will have even younger peers in heaven. Saint John Bosco's feast day is on 31st January, Dominic Savio's on 9th March.

Saint Louis Maria Grignion de Montfort (1673–1716)
This French saint is best known for his book *True Devotion to the Blessed Virgin* and for his society of priests, the Company of Mary, better known as the Monfortorians. He also founded a sisterhood called the Sisters of Wisdom. From childhood he was devoted to prayer before the Blessed Sacrament. At nineteen he walked to Paris from Montfort in Britanny to follow his theological studies, and gave

away all his money and swapped his clothes with beggars on the way. He was ordained at twenty-seven but didn't find his true vocation, preaching, till he was thirty-two – only a decade or so before his death. His whole life was conspicuous for virtues difficult for modern degeneracy to comprehend: constant prayer, love of the poor, poverty carried to an extreme degree, joy in humiliations and persecutions.

The Monfortorian Fathers have a large house, formerly a seminary, behind the Basilica in *Avenida Beato Nuno* facing the *Rua dos Monfortinos*. St. Louis' feast day is on 28th April.

Saint Vincent de Paul (1581–1660)

The son of a peasant farmer, he was ordained at twenty and aspired to no more than a life of clerical ease when he was captured at sea by Turks, taken to Tunis, and sold as a slave. After two years he escaped but his life thereafter was marked by an almost super-human compassion for the poor and the suffering. The list of his achievements fills volumes and after three hundred and fifty years he still seems to exert an almost physical presence in French Catholicism. It was said of him that he was sharp-tempered and lacking in external advantages yet, through grace, his kindness, prudence and benign influence on every sphere of life he touched is legendary. His zeal for souls knew no limits; he took all occasions as opportunities to exercise it.

Vincent de Paul founded the Congregation of the Mission for priests and, with St Louise de Marillac,

the Daughers of Charity. The St Vincent de Paul
Society, a charitable organisation of laymen so well
known in many parishes, was founded in Paris in 1833
by a student, Frédéric Ozanam. In 1948 the saint's life
was the subject of a film by Bernard Luc and Jean
Anouilh called *Monsieur Vincent*. The Sisters of St
Vincent de Paul have a house in the Rua San Vincente
de Paul almost opposite the Domus Pracis building.
His feast day is on 27th September.

Saint Simon Stock (c. 1165–1265)
The only Englishman to be represented in Fatima,
this Carmelite might also be nominated as the patron
of geriatrics. Almost nothing is known of him for
certain until he was elected sixth General of the
Carmelites at the first chapter held at Aylesford in
England. He was, at the time, around eighty years old
and he lived to be a hundred. During his generalship
the order became widespread in southern and western
Europe, especially in England. He wisely founded
houses in the university towns, Oxford, Cambridge,
Paris and Bologna, which was invaluable for the training of younger members and the growth of the
institution.

In spite of its success it appears that the order was
greatly oppressed, both by the secular clergy and the
other orders. The Carmelites prayed ardently to their
Patroness, the Blessed Virgin. It is recorded that Our
Holy Mother appeared to Simon with the scapular of
the Order in Her hand and told him to apply fearlessly
to the Pope for redress. (This was done and a Papal

229

Bull offering Innocent IV's protection for the Carmelites dated 13th January 1252 is still extant.) At the same time Our Lady is said to have handed him the scapular saying, **'This shall be the privilege for you and for all Carmelites, that anyone dying in this habit shall be saved.'**

It was a customn at the time for an order to present its habit to benefactors and friends of high rank. When Our Lady's promise to Simon Stock became known it is understandable that everybody wanted a Carmelite scapular which is doubtless why it was reduced in size to the scapular we know today.

He is represented in Fatima because of the strong Carmelite presence in the town and because of his part in the introduction of the Brown Scapular which Our Lady was holding in Her appearance as Our Lady of Carmel, seen by Lucia, Francisco and Jacinta during the Miracle of the Sun on 13th October 1917.

The surname Stock is not found attributed to this saint till a century after his death. On account of his English birth he was formerly better known as Simon Anglus. His feast day is 16th May.

Saint Ignatius Loyola (1491–1556)
As a young Basque soldier Ignatius (Iñigo), the future founder of the Jesuits, was wounded while defending Pamplona against the French. He spent his convalescence reading spiritual books and determined to give his life wholly to God's service. After a year in retirement which he spent in intense prayer and during which he started to write his *Spiritual Exercises*,

Ignatius made a pilgrimage to Jerusalem and then gave himself to study.

While reading for a Master of Arts degree at the University of Paris he became the inspiration for a group of students – one of them was Francis Xavier – who, some years later in Italy offered their services to Pope Paul III. They were ordained and formed into a regular religious order with the usual vows and an added one of being at the Pope's disposal at any time, anywhere. At this time Ignatius was fifty. For the remaining years of his life he directed the order from Rome and saw it grow from the original ten to over a thousand, involving itself in education, the missions, and meeting the challenge of the Protestant Reformation. His feast day is kept on 31st July.

Saint Paul of the Cross (1694–1775)
His name was Paul Francis Danei and he came from Piedmont in Italy. At twenty he volunteered for the Venetian army but soon realised he was not meant for a military life. He gave himself over to a life of prayer and austerity. In his mid-thirties he had a mystical communication which convinced him that he was called to found a congregation of missioners whose life and work was to be specially centred on the Saviour's cross and passion – hence the Passionists. Despite many initial difficulties the congregation finally flourished and at Paul's death a convent of enclosed Passionist nuns had also been established. Like Louis de Montfort his feast is on 28th April.

Paul of the Cross always showed a particular interest in bringing England back to the faith. The leader of the first Passionists to work there, the tireless missioner Dominic Barberi – he died in 1849 – the man who received John Henry, later Cardinal, Newman into the Church, was beatified in 1963.

Saint John of the Cross (1542–1591)

His name was Juan Yepes and he was born in the Avila area of Spain. He became a Carmelite friar and in 1568 joined the reform of the Order started by Teresa of Avila. He was imprisoned by the Carmelites opposed to the reform in 1577 and subjected to inhuman treatment. After nine months he escaped. He was appointed to various offices among the reformed friars and during this time wrote his books which have become classics of mystical literature. Towards the end of his life he was removed from office and banished to a remote friary where he was again treated oppressively. Only after his death did he receive the recognition due to the co-founder of the Carmelite Reform and a major spiritual writer. He was named a Doctor of the Church by Pope Pius XI in 1926. His feast is observed on 24th November.

Both the original Carmelite Friars and the Reform (discalced – literally 'without shoes' though this is no longer so) have houses in Fatima. The hotel, Casa Beato Nuno, belongs to the original friars and the discalced are along the road a little way with an entrance in Rua Nossa Senhora do Carmo 2.

Saint Beatrice de Silva (d. 1st September 1490)
Beatrice was a member of the house of Portalegre and descended from the Portuguese royal family. She was the sister of João Mendez de Silva (1420–1482) better known as Blessed Amadeus of Portugal who, like St Anthony before him, became a Franciscan and went to Italy.

She accompanied the Portuguese Princess Isabel to Spain when she married John II of Castile. There the great beauty of Beatrice aroused the jealousy of her royal mistress and she was imprisoned for three days without food.

After a vision of Our Lady, who was wearing the blue mantle and white dress of the Conception order, which she was later to found, Beatrice entered a Dominican convent in Toledo without, however, taking vows with the order. She lived there for thirty years, being specially honoured and frequently visited by Queen Isabel, the same monarch who sent Columbus on his voyage of discovery. This Isabel also helped Beatrice to found her order in honour of the Immaculate Conception which at first lived by the Cistercian rule and later adopted that of St Clare. It was approved by Innocent VIII in 1489. Beatrice died ten days before its solemn inauguration.

The order has a conent and old people's home, Lar de Beatrice de Silva, at No.8 Rua da Anjo behind the Santuário bookshop. Her feast is celebrated on 1st September.

Biography

Books

Baker, G. L., *The Finger of God is Here*, St Paul's, 1961.

Cacella, Joseph, *The Wonders of Fatima*, New York, 1948.

Cirrincione, Msgr Joseph A., *Fatima's Message for Our Times*, Dominican Nuns of the Perpetual Rosary, 1992.

De Marchi, Fr. John IMC., *Fatima: From the Beginning*, tr. from Portuguese by I.M. Kingsbury, Missões Consolata-Fatima.

Dos Santos, Lucia, *Fatima: in Lucia's Own Words*, Fr. Louis Kondor, SDV (ed), tr. Dominican Nuns of Perpetual Rosary.

Dos Santos, Lucia, *Fatima: in Lucia's Own Words* II, tr. Domincan Nuns of Perpetual Rosary.

Evaristo, Carlos, *Two Hours with Sister Lucia*, Portugal, 1997.

Foley, Donal Anthony, *Apparitions of Mary; their Meaning in History*, CTS., London, 2000.

Galamba de Oliveira, José, *Jacinta of Fatima*, Sydney, 1945.

Haffert, J.M., *Meet the Witnesses*, Washington N.J., 1961.

Johnston, Francis, *Fatima, The Great Sign*, Illinois, 1980.

Leite, Fr. Fernando SJ., *Francisco of Fatima: Our Lady's Little Shepherd*, and *Jacinta of Fatima: Our Lady's Little Shepherdess*, (Pamphlets for children) tr. Dominican Nuns of Perpetual Rosary, Fatima, 1980.

Leite, Fr. Fernando SJ, *Francisco of Fatima*, A.O. Braga (ed.) tr. Dominican Nuns of the Perpetual Rosary, 1999.

McGlynn, Fr. Thomas OP, *Vision of Fatima*, Skeffington & Sons, London, 1951.

Madigan, Leo, *What Happened at Fatima*, CTS., London, 2000.

Madigan, Leo, *Fatima – Highway of Hope*, (photographs by Francisco de Almeida Dias), ELO, Mafra, Portugal, 2000.

Martindale C.C., *The Message of Fatima*, London, 1950.

Martins, Fr. Antonio Maria SJ, *Fatima and Our Salvation*, tr. Dominican Nuns of the Perpetual Rosary, Augustine Publishing.

Norton, Mabel, *Eyewitness at Fatima*, C.J. Fallon, Dublin, 1950.

Ryan, Fr. Finbar, *Our Lady of Fatima*, Dublin, 1939.

Tindal-Robertson, Timothy, *Fatima, Russia & Pope John Paul II*, (3rd, enlarged, edn.), Gracewing, Leominster, 1998.

Tindal-Robertson, Timothy, *Message of Fatima*, Catholic Truth Society, London, 1998.

Walsh Fr. W.T., *Our Lady of Fatima*, New York, 1947.

Index

KEY TO MAP OF FATIMA

A Centro Comercial
Religious Articles Supermarket
Ph: 249 53 23 75

B Dom Gonçalo (p. 186)
Restaurant, Estalagem
Ph: 249 53 93 30

C Postulation Centre
Rua de São Pedro
Ph: 249 53 22 14

D Solar da Marta (p. 185)
Hotel, Cafeteria
Ph: 249 53 11 52

E Rosmaninho Café (p. 185)
Villa Fatima Hotel
Ph: 249 53 90 10

F Museum of Sacred Art (p. 180ff)
Rua Francisco Marto
Ph: 249 53 29 15

G Pius XII Convent
Dominican Sisters of Perpetual
Rosary
Perpetual Adoration
English Books
Ph: 249 53 21 66

H Tia Alice
Restaurant (p. 186)
Ph: 249 53 17 37

I O Truão
Restaurant (p. 186)
Ph: 249 52 15 42

1. Rotondo de Norte
2. Petrol Station
3. Police Station
4. Bus Station
5. Stª Luzia, Moita
6. Poor Clare Convent
7. Carmelite Convent
8. Chemist
9. Post Office
10. Paul VI Centre
11. São João, Lomba
12. Market
13. Rotondo do Sul
14. Hungarian Via Cruz
15. Hungarian Calvary
16. Valinhos
17. Aljustrel
18. Tourist Information

Map of Fatima © José Manuel Braga